Harcourt

Writing

Grade 3

ISBN 978-0-5442-6847-0

1 2 3 4 5 6 7 8 9 10 XXXX 22 21 20 19 18 17 16 15 14 13

4500000000 B C D E F G

Core Skills Writing

GRADE 3

Table of Contents

Table of Contents
Core Skills Writing, Grade 3

Introduction

Writing is one of the core skills necessary for success in school and in life. The better writer a person is, the better that person can communicate with others. Good writing is a skill acquired through guidance, practice, and self-evaluation. This book provides guidance for success in different writing formats. This book also provides many opportunities for writing practice. Finally, this book encourages writers to examine their own work, as well as that of their peers, and judge its qualities and flaws.

Clear writing and clear speaking are products of clear thinking. Clear thinking is a product of good organization of ideas. Good organization is a product of careful planning. One good way to plan is through graphic organizers.

- In this book, different kinds of graphic organizers are provided for students to plan their writing.

- These organizers appeal to the multiple intelligences. They provide students with a visual and tactile approach in their writing.

- Some graphic organizers guide students through specific steps in the writing process. The organizers help them focus on the elements of good writing.

- Other organizers help students organize their writing so as to ensure a successful writing experience.

Organization

This book is divided into four units. Each unit builds upon earlier units. Using this scaffolded approach, students will find that writing becomes like construction.

- **Unit 1: Laying the Foundation** addresses the basic process of writing, such as parts of speech, writing traits, and the process of writing.

- **Unit 2: Building Sentences** emphasizes the act of writing. Writers first deal with the main idea of a sentence, then expand sentences by adding other parts of speech.

- **Unit 3: Building Paragraphs** focuses on the structure and content of a well-written paragraph. Writers also learn about revising, proofreading, publishing, and self- and peer-evaluation in this unit.

- **Unit 4: Writing Forms** provides guidance and practice writing in different formats such as narration, description, persuasion, opinion, and short stories.

Write Away

For too many students, writing is a struggle or a pain. They may not realize the benefits of being a good writer, or they may not care. This book tries to reach out to all writers with an approach that allows students to "see" their writing in a new light. Writing does not have to be a chore. It can be fun. Students just have to be reminded that good writing can be their golden ticket to success in school and life.

Features

The title clearly identifies the skill.

Examples model the skill.

Bullets highlight important points of the skill.

Students creatively apply the skill in **WRITE AWAY.**

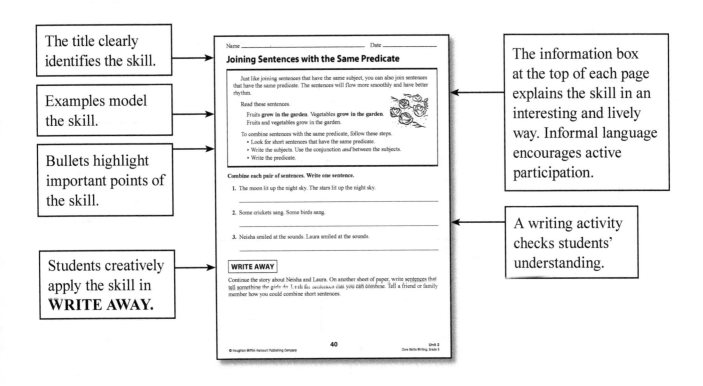

The information box at the top of each page explains the skill in an interesting and lively way. Informal language encourages active participation.

A writing activity checks students' understanding.

Self-assessments guide students through the writing process.

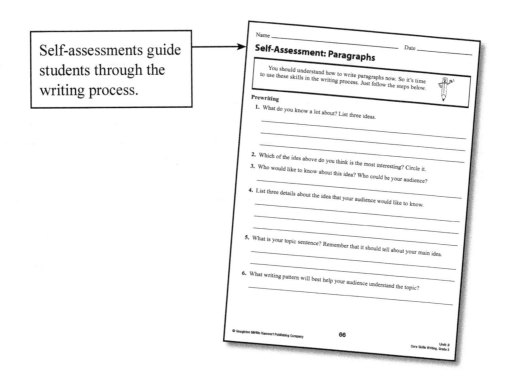

Skills Correlation

Skill	Page
Types of Writing	
Opinion Paragraph	92, 93, 94, 95
Introduction; Organizational Structure	92, 93, 94, 95
Reasons That Support the Opinion	92, 94, 95
Linking Words and Phrases	92
Concluding Statement or Section	92, 93
Informative/Explanatory Texts	80, 81, 82, 83
Topic Development with Facts, Definitions, and Details	80
Illustrations to Aid in Comprehension	80, 83
Linking Words and Phrases	81, 82
Concluding Statement or Section	80
Narrative Paragraph	68, 69
Situation, Narrator, Characters, Event Sequence	68, 69
Dialogue and Description	69
Temporal Words and Phrases	68, 69
Conclusion	68, 69
Short Research Project	96, 97, 98
Recall Information from Experiences; Gather Information from Print and Digital Sources; Take Notes and Categorize Information	96, 97, 98
Journal	4
Person Description	70, 71
Place Description	72, 73
Thing Description	74, 75
How-to Paragraph	76, 77
Persuasive Paragraph	78, 79
Compare and Contrast Paragraph	84, 85
Poem	86, 87
Friendly Letter	88, 89
Book Report	90, 91
Biography	99, 100
Short Story	27, 30, 101, 102, 103, 104, 105, 106
Writing Process	
Development and Organization, Task, Purpose	60, 68, 69, 80, 81, 82, 83, 92, 93, 94, 95, 96, 97, 98, 118, 119, 120, 121, 122, 123, 124
Voice	15, 30, 59, 69, 71
Planning, Revising, and Editing	12, 13, 48, 60, 61, 62, 63, 64, 65, 67, 73, 75, 106, 108, 109, 114, 115, 118, 119, 120, 121, 122, 123, 124
Publishing/Publishing Using Technology	13, 48, 67, 83, 85, 89, 91, 95, 98, 100, 106, 116, 117
Composition	
Paragraph Structure	49, 50, 51, 52, 53, 54, 55

Skills Correlation, continued

Skill	Page
Vocabulary	
Synonyms	36
Antonyms	37
Homophones	38
Sentences	
Recognizing Sentences and Sentence Types	20, 23, 24, 25, 26, 27
Subject and Predicates	20, 21, 26, 39, 40, 44
Combining Sentences	39, 40, 41, 42
Expanding Sentences	32, 33, 35
Run-on Sentences	45
Grammar and Usage	
Nouns	5, 28
Verbs	7, 29, 30, 31
Pronouns	6
Adjectives	8, 32, 33
Adverbs	9, 35, 44
Prepositions	10, 44
Conjunctions	11, 39, 40, 41, 42
Capitalization and Punctuation	
Capitalization: First Word in Sentence	20
Capitalization: Proper Nouns	5
Capitalization: Parts of a Letter	88
End Punctuation	20, 23, 24, 25, 26
Commas	27, 41, 42, 43, 56, 88
Quotation Marks	27

Writing Rubric

Score of 4

The student:

- <u>clearly</u> follows the writing process,
- demonstrates an understanding of the purpose for writing,
- expresses creativity,
- presents the main idea and supports it with relevant detail,
- uses paragraphs to organize main ideas and supporting ideas under the umbrella of a thesis statement,
- presents content in a logical order and sequence,
- uses variety in sentence beginnings and length,
- chooses the correct writing pattern and form to communicate ideas clearly,
- clearly portrays feelings through voice and word choice,
- uses language appropriate to the writing task, such as language rich in sensory details,
- uses vocabulary to suit purpose and audience,
- summarizes main ideas when appropriate, such as in a persuasive paragraph or response to literature,
- establishes and defends a position in a persuasive paragraph, and
- has few or no errors in the standard rules of English grammar, punctuation, capitalization, and spelling.

Score of 3

The student:

- <u>generally</u> follows the criteria described above, and
- has some errors in the standard rules of English grammar, punctuation, capitalization, and spelling, but not enough to impair a reader's comprehension.

Score of 2

The student:

- <u>marginally</u> follows the criteria described above, and
- has several errors in the standard rules of English grammar, punctuation, capitalization, and spelling, which may impair a reader's comprehension.

Score of 1

The student:

- <u>fails</u> to follow the criteria described above, and
- has many errors in the standard rules of English grammar, punctuation, capitalization, and spelling that impair a reader's comprehension.

Why Write?

Many students say they don't like to write. They would rather talk to share stories and information. But writing is much like talking. When you write or talk, you use ideas. You use words and sentences. The goal is the same. When you talk or write, you are communicating with others.

Sometimes it is better to write than to talk.

- When you write, you can think about your ideas before putting them on paper. When you talk, you might say something you don't really mean.
- When you write, you can organize your ideas ahead of time. When you talk, you might not clearly explain an idea.
- When you write, your ideas will last on paper forever. When you talk, your ideas will disappear into the air.
- Writing can take your place when you are not there to talk.

Writing can be fun, too. Just think, in twenty or thirty years, you can read something you wrote in the third grade. Won't that be funny?

Darken the circle by the answer that best completes each sentence.

1. When you write, you can _think_ about your ideas before putting them on paper.

   Ⓐ talk   Ⓑ sleep   Ⓒ think

2. Writing takes your _place_ when you are not there to talk.

   Ⓐ place   Ⓑ lunch   Ⓒ ideas

WRITE AWAY

Sometimes, the hardest part about writing is getting the idea. At times like that, you should write about things that interest you. Complete the Writing Interest Survey on pages 112–113. It may help you get an idea of some things you could write about.

1

What to Write

There are many reasons that you write. You might write a thank-you letter to a family member. You might write directions telling how to get to your house. You may not realize it, but you have made three decisions before your pencil touches the paper.

- You have chosen an **audience**.
- You have chosen a **purpose**.
- You have chosen how to **organize** the writing.

The audience, purpose, and organization often help you choose the kind of writing you will do.

Who is your audience? Your audience will be the ones who read what you write. The audience could be a neighbor, an editor of a newspaper, or even you! But before you begin writing, you should think about your audience. Here are some questions to help you.

- Who will read what I write?
- What do I have to say to the reader?
- Am I writing about my feelings or about facts?
- Will my writing be funny or serious?
- What will make the reader keep reading what I wrote?

Write the name of a possible audience for each piece of writing.

1. a book report

_____

2. a speech about a community problem

_____

3. an invitation to a party

_____

4. a poem about a dancing duck

_____

WRITE AWAY

Think of a time you did something special. Imagine writing a letter to a grandparent telling him or her about the event. Now imagine writing a letter to a five-year-old child. Would you use the same words? Why or why not? How would the letter be different? Discuss your ideas with a friend or family member. On another sheet of paper, write sentences telling your ideas.

2

What to Write, continued

What is your purpose for writing? When you write, you have a purpose, or reason, for writing. The purpose can help you choose the form of writing, too. Writers have four main purposes:

- to **express**, or tell, their feelings or ideas (diary, journal)
- to **entertain** others so they are pleased (story, poem, joke)
- to **persuade** others so they think or act a certain way (speech, book review)
- to **inform**, or tell information (report, list, research paper)

How will you organize your writing? The way you organize, or arrange, the ideas in your writing affects how the writing looks. It affects the form you will use. Short stories, poems, letters, and lists are examples of different forms of writing.

What form will you use when you write? Your audience and your purpose can help you choose the form. This book presents some of the forms you can use to write what you have to say.

What purpose would you use to write each of the following? Write *express*, *entertain*, *persuade*, or *inform*.

1. a television commercial

_____

2. your feelings for a pet

_____

3. a funny story about washing a dog

_____

4. a science report

_____

WRITE AWAY

Imagine that you want to spend the night at a friend's house. You need to ask permission. Who would be your audience? What purpose could you use?

Audience: _____   Purpose: _____

3

Name _____ Date _____

Keeping a Journal

Jour is a French word that means "day." A writer uses a **journal** to keep a record of daily events. In a journal, you can record what you do or how you feel. You can write stories or poems, too. You can even draw pictures. The pictures can show what you see or how you feel, just like words. The pictures can also go along with the words you write. Here's a sample of a journal.

February 5

I woke up and found that it had snowed all night! The ground was covered in white. It was very exciting because it doesn't snow here often. I got my sled and rushed to the park. It has a big hill that is perfect for sledding. All my friends were already gliding down the hill. It was a great day!

You can make your journal by doing these things.

- Write the date.
- Write about important things that happened that day.
- Write poems or stories about the events.
- Draw a picture about important things that you saw.
- Draw a picture to go along with your words.

You don't have to use complete sentences or worry about spelling and end marks. It's your journal. It's your personal writing place. No one has to see it except you. Journals can be funny to read when you get older.

Write a short journal entry about something that happened to you today. Tell why it is important to you.

Date _____

_____

_____

WRITE AWAY

Start your own journal. You can use notebook paper or the graphic organizer on page 107. Write about your feelings and ideas. Write poems and stories. Draw a picture. Remember that a journal is just for you!

Parts of Speech: Nouns

We say and write words to communicate with others. Each word belongs to a special group, or part of speech. Learning the different parts of speech can help you become a better writer.

One of the most important parts of speech is a **noun**. A noun names things. A noun is a word that names a person, place, or thing.

- A **common noun** names any person, place, or thing (boy, library, book). It begins with a lowercase letter.
- A **proper noun** names a special person, place, or thing (Pablo, New York, Statue of Liberty). It begins with a capital letter.

Write at least one common noun and one proper noun that are part of each group.

1. park _____

_____

2. library _____

_____

3. game _____

_____

WRITE AWAY

Go on a noun hunt! Look around you and write the names of 15 nouns you see. Be sure to include some proper nouns, too.

_____

_____

_____

_____

_____

5

Parts of Speech: Pronouns

You just learned about nouns. A noun is a word that names a person, place, or thing. Now you will learn about another part of speech— a **pronoun**. A pronoun can take the place of a noun. You use pronouns so that you will not repeat words.

Sentence with Nouns	The **crab** pinched **Jill's** toe.
Sentence with Pronouns	**It** hurt **her** toe.

Here are the pronouns.

I	you	he	she	it	we	they
mine	yours	his	hers	its	ours	theirs
my	your	her	our	their		

Write at least two nouns that are part of each group. Then write a pronoun that could take the place of each noun.

1. your bedroom _____

_____

2. family _____

_____

3. books _____

_____

WRITE AWAY

Write the names of ten nouns you see. Then write a pronoun that might take the place of each.

_____

_____

_____

_____

6

Parts of Speech: Verbs

A **verb** is another important part of speech. A verb shows action or a state of being. All sentences have verbs.

Eva **hugs** her pig.
The pig **is** pink.

Verbs are also used to tell when something is happening. The time a verb tells is called **tense**. A verb can be present tense, past tense, or future tense.

- A **present tense** verb tells what is happening now.
- A **past tense** verb tells what happened in the past.
- A **future tense** verb tells what will happen in the future.

present	past	future
yell	yelled	will yell

Write two verbs that could belong to each group.

1. making breakfast _____

2. a favorite sport _____

3. doing chores _____

WRITE AWAY

What are some verbs that tell actions you can do with water? (swim, cook) Write a list of all the verbs you can think of that tell actions you can do with water.

_____

_____

_____

_____

_____

7

Parts of Speech: Adjectives

An **adjective** is another part of speech. It describes a noun or a pronoun. It tells how something looks or feels. It also tells how many.

The **two little, fuzzy gray** mice hid from **one large, scary** cat.

Writers use adjectives to make their writing more lively. Adjectives help readers understand what a writer is saying.

Write at least three adjectives that describe each noun.

1. snow _____

_____

2. strawberries _____

_____

3. skunks _____

_____

WRITE AWAY

On another sheet of paper, draw a picture. You can use a pencil, a pen, or crayons. Then write adjectives on the lines below to describe your picture.

_____

_____

_____

_____

_____

8

Parts of Speech: Adverbs

An **adverb** is another important part of speech. It describes a verb, adjective, or another adverb. Most adverbs show where, when, or how.

Elly's **very** big dog **often** barks **loudly here**.

Writers like to use adverbs. Adverbs help readers clearly understand what a writer is saying.

Write at least two adverbs that could be used to describe each word.

1. worked _____

_____

2. ran _____

_____

3. screamed _____

_____

WRITE AWAY

Imagine that you are at a soccer game. Write at least ten adverbs that you could use to describe the action on the field and in the crowd.

_____

_____

_____

_____

_____

_____

Parts of Speech: Prepositions

A **preposition** is another part of speech. A preposition is a word that shows place or time.

The shovel is **in** the ground.

Here are some other prepositions.

above	across	after	at	before	behind	below
for	from	in	into	near	of	on
over	past	through	to	under	until	with

Writers use prepositions to give more information.

Look at the picture. Use prepositions to tell where people, animals, and things are.

_____

_____

_____

_____

_____

_____

_____

_____

_____

WRITE AWAY

On another sheet of paper, draw a picture of an obstacle course using materials around you, such as chairs, tables, and toys. Write directions to tell how to move through the course.

10

Parts of Speech: Conjunctions

A **conjunction** is another part of speech. A conjunction is a word that connects words or groups of words.

Jay **and** Sara are coming, **but** they will be late.

Here are some conjunctions.

also	and	because	but	for
nor	or	so	yet	

Writers often use conjunctions to make their writing more interesting.

Answer the questions using complete sentences. Use conjunctions.

1. What are your two favorite sports? _____

_____

2. What do you dislike doing? Why? _____

_____

3. What activities can you choose to do later today? Name at least two.

_____

_____

WRITE AWAY

Think about the conjunctions *and* and *so*. When should writers use the words? Discuss your ideas with a friend or family member. Then write a sentence or two telling your ideas.

_____

_____

_____

11

The Writing Process

Looking at a clean, white sheet of paper can be scary. Sometimes you can't think of anything to write. But you don't need to worry! Many famous writers have felt like you. Luckily, there are some steps that you can follow to help you fill that paper.

Here are the five steps that many writers follow. They are briefly introduced now to give you an idea of the writing process. You'll learn more about each one later.

Prewriting

Prewriting is sometimes called **brainstorming.** It is the step where you think about what you are writing and why. You choose a purpose, or a reason, for your writing. You make a list of your ideas and choose a **topic.** A topic is what you are writing about. Then you organize the ideas so that they make sense. Many writers use webs to help them list the **details,** or facts and information, they will include. The Prewriting Survey on pages 108–109 can help you plan your writing.

Drafting

In the **drafting** step, writers put their ideas on paper. They write words, ideas, and sentences. There are often many mistakes in this kind of writing. But that's OK! You just want to get all of your ideas down on paper. You can fix mistakes later.

Imagine that a family member is serving a vegetable that you do not like. You decide to write about it in your journal. Use the organizer below to help you prewrite.

Nouns I might use: _____

Verbs I might use: _____

Adjectives I might use: _____

Adverbs I might use: _____

WRITE AWAY

In a journal or on another sheet of paper, write about the vegetable that you dislike.

The Writing Process, continued

Revising

In the **revising** step, you read your draft. You should check to make sure that your writing makes sense and your purpose is clear. You might take out or add details. You can move ideas around. You can add words to make the writing clearer. You might even ask someone else to read your work and give you suggestions to improve the writing.

Proofreading

It is important to **proofread**, or look at, your work for mistakes before you publish it. The **editing** step is where you correct your mistakes. Read your work once for capital letters. Read it a second time for end marks and commas. Read it a third time for spelling. You can use the Proofreading Checklist on page 114 as a guide. A list of Proofreading Marks can be found on page 115.

Publishing

Publishing is fun. During this stage, you make a clean copy of your writing. You can handwrite it or type it on the computer. You can add pictures if you wish. Sometimes you might make a cover and a title page. Now the work is ready to share!

Read the steps in the writing process. Write numbers *1* through *5* to show the correct order.

_____ Begin writing. Don't worry about mistakes!

_____ Check your spelling and grammar.

_____ Choose something to write about and make notes.

_____ Make a clean copy of your writing to share with others.

_____ Read to make sure that your writing makes sense.

WRITE AWAY

Think about different ways to publish your writing. Discuss your ideas with a friend or family member. On another sheet of paper, write about your ideas.

13

The Writing Traits

Every time you write, you have a reason, or purpose, for writing. You might want to make readers laugh. You might want to share some information. You might even want to get the readers to think the way that you do. There are seven **writing traits,** or skills, which will help you become a great writer.

Ideas

Ideas are the thoughts and pictures you form in your mind. They are very important. So you want to share these ideas with others. When you write, you need to make sure that the readers understand your message. You want them to be interested in your message, too. To meet these goals, your ideas need to make sense. You should include many details that will make the ideas clear.

Organization

The **organization** of your writing is the way that you group ideas and details. First, you should choose the correct form of writing. Letters, e-mail messages, stories, and journals are some writing forms that you can choose. Next, your writing should have a beginning, a middle, and an end. The ideas should also be written in order so that they are easy to follow. Finally, check the first sentence. Does it grab the reader's attention? If so, the reader will keep reading. That's important!

Write a word from the box to complete each sentence.

idea	sentence	organization	traits

1. The first _____ should grab a reader's attention.

2. Seven writing _____ will help you become a great writer.

3. You should include details to make the _____ clear.

4. The way that you group ideas and details in writing is _____.

WRITE AWAY

How is a letter like an e-mail message? How is it different? Write about your ideas on another sheet of paper. Discuss your ideas with a friend or family member.

The Writing Traits, continued

Voice

    When you are happy, you smile. You speak more quickly and use kind words. When you are angry, you might shout loudly. You have a frown on your face, and you use mean words. Most likely, the person next to you clearly understands what you are feeling.

    As a writer, you will want to let the reader know your feelings, too. You can share your feelings through the words you choose. This skill is called **voice**. To share a happy feeling, you will write about happy ideas and choose happy words. For an angry feeling, you will write about angry ideas and choose angry words.

Word Choice

    You learned how words help a reader feel a certain way. **Word choice** is important in other ways, too. You want to make sure that the reader clearly understands what you are saying or describing. You can do this by using words that relate to five senses. The reader should be able to read, hear, taste, smell, and touch your ideas by reading your words. You could also choose specific words and strong action words to explain an idea. Did you see a <u>dog</u> or a <u>fuzzy, white poodle</u>? Did the squirrel <u>run</u> or <u>scamper</u> up the tree?

Write a word from the box to complete each sentence.

words	senses	voice

1. Words that relate to the five _____ can tell a reader what you see, hear, taste, smell, and touch.

2. Choosing exact _____ can explain an idea.

3. You are able to make the reader feel the way you do when you use the trait

    of _____.

WRITE AWAY

What are some words that you could use to describe a puppy? Write words that relate to all five senses on another sheet of paper.

The Writing Traits, continued

Sentence Fluency

A **sentence** is a group of words that tells a complete thought. When your writing has **sentence fluency**, the sentences are ordered so that the text flows smoothly and has a rhythm. You can achieve this by writing long and short sentences and by writing sentences with different patterns. Some sentences might begin with a noun. Others might begin with a preposition.

Conventions

The **conventions** are the rules of grammar and spelling. You want to catch your mistakes. Does every sentence begin with a capital letter? Does each sentence have the correct end mark? Are all words spelled correctly?

Presentation

Presentation is the way that the words and pictures look on the page. You want to make sure the work looks neat and clean so it is easy to read. The pictures should show the most important ideas. Don't forget the title! The title is the first thing readers see. It needs to be interesting so that a reader will say, "Wow! This sounds interesting. I can't wait to read this!"

You can use these writing traits throughout the writing process. Doing so will help you become a better writer. You can also use the Writing Traits Checklist on pages 110–111 to help you. The list is easy to read. It can help you focus on each of the traits as you write. Before long, your work will be better than ever!

Write a word from the box to complete each sentence.

presentation	conventions	title	fluency

1. The way the words and pictures look on the paper is the trait of _____.

2. A good _____ needs to be interesting so that a reader wants to read your work.

3. The _____ are the rules of grammar and spelling.

4. The way you order words in sentences is sentence _____.

Basic Rules of Writing

Now that you know about the writing process, let's take a look at some other rules that will help you write more easily and clearly.

Write what you know.

Write about the things that interest you. You probably already know many facts and details about the things you are interested in, so you will have a lot to say. You will like the topic, too. You can use the Prewriting Survey on pages 108–109 to help you think about some topics that interest you.

Make a list of what you need to know about your topic.

Make a list or web that shows the facts and details of your topic before you begin writing. This way you can find out if you are missing important information. Then you can look for the details or ask someone to help you.

Make sure your topic is the right size.

It is important to choose a topic that is the right size. When a topic is too big, it is hard to include all the important facts. It is hard to write about a topic that is too small, too. You will not have enough information in your writing.

Draw a picture before you begin to write.

If you are telling about an event, it is helpful to draw a picture before you write. It will help you remember to include the details about people, places, and other things that are important to the story. These details often help the reader feel as if he or she is there.

Write a word from the box to complete each sentence.

interest	topic	picture	list

1. Make a _____ or web that shows facts and details about your topic.

2. Write about things that _____ you.

3. A _____ can help you remember to include details that are important to a story.

4. Choose a _____ that is not too big or too small.

17

Basic Rules of Writing, continued

Use your notes and lists as you write.

In the prewriting stage, you make notes, lists, and webs to help organize your ideas. You should look at them often when you write your draft. They will help you remember all the ideas that you wanted to include in your writing. They will help you stick to the topic, too. All of your details will tell only about the topic.

Start by writing the part that you know best.

Sometimes you may not know how you want to start your writing. You might find it helpful to begin writing the part that you know best. Once there is something on the paper, the rest of the words often come easily.

Reread your writing. Add details to make your writing come alive.

When you read your draft, look for things that a reader might not understand or things the reader would want to know more about. For example, if you are telling a story about a dog named Spot, readers would probably want to know how he got his name.

Read your writing out loud.

Read your draft out loud. It can help you find the parts that do not make sense or do not flow smoothly.

Write a word or words from the box to complete each sentence.

out loud	stick	best	draft

1. Start by writing the part you know _____.

2. Read your _____ to look for things that a reader might not understand.

3. Looking at your notes, lists, and webs will help you _____ to the topic.

4. Reading your draft _____ can help you find parts that do not make sense.

18

Basic Rules of Writing, continued

Find a great title by using words that are in your writing.

Reread the writing to focus on words that would make a great and exciting title. The title should sound interesting to a reader so that he or she will want to read on.

Read the finished writing to look for mistakes.

When you proofread, you take a final look at your writing to check for mistakes. Read it once for capital letters. Read it a second time for end marks and commas. Read it a third time to look for words you do not know how to spell. Circle those words and then look in a dictionary to check them. Use the Proofreading Checklist on page 114 to find common mistakes.

Make a cover and title page.

At long last, your writing is complete. You should be proud! You can show off your work with a cover. The picture on the cover should tell the **main idea,** or most important idea, of the writing. Don't forget that you are the author, so write your name on it, too! Then make a cover page that also includes the title and your name.

Write a word from the box to complete each sentence.

mistakes	picture	title

1. Reread the writing to focus on words that would make a great _____.

2. Read the finished writing several times to look for spelling, capitalization, and

    punctuation _____.

3. The _____ on the cover should tell the main idea of the writing.

WRITE AWAY

How will you use the basic rules of writing to improve your writing in the future? Write a list of ideas on another sheet of paper.

What Is a Sentence?

A sentence is a group of words that tells a complete thought. Every sentence begins with a capital letter and ends with an end mark. A sentence has two main parts, a **subject** and a **predicate**.

- The subject tells who or what the sentence is about. Nouns or pronouns are used as the subject. A sentence can have more than one subject.

  Birds fly.   **Boys and girls** play.   **The sun** shines brightly.

- The predicate tells what the subject is or does. Verbs are used in the predicate.

  Birds **fly**.   Boys and girls **play**.   The sun **shines brightly**.

Write a word or words on the line to make each sentence complete.

1. _____ shouts.

2. _____ reads.

3. Ron and Dan _____.

4. The toy _____.

WRITE AWAY

Write four sentence parts. Include either a subject or a predicate. Draw a line for the other part. Have a friend or family member complete the sentences. Check to make sure the sentence is complete.

_____

_____

_____

_____

_____

The Main Idea of a Sentence

Remember that a sentence has two main parts, the subject and the predicate.

subject

⌐The butterflies⌐fly in the sky.⌐

predicate

Each sentence also has a main idea. The main idea is made with the noun and verb. It is important to know what the main idea of each sentence is. It will help you write clear sentences. A graphic organizer can help you identify the main idea of a sentence. A bar separates the noun from the verb.

butterflies	fly
noun	**verb**

Complete each sentence. Then use the graphic organizer to show the main idea. Write the noun and verb.

1. The fluffy cat _____.

         ——————+——————

2. _____ happily chirped.

         ——————+——————

3. _____ slithered in the grass.

         ——————+——————

WRITE AWAY

Think of three animals. What do they do? Write sentences about the animals and their actions.

_____

_____

_____

_____

21

Present Tense Verbs

Some sentences tell about actions that are happening now. These sentences are written in the **present tense**. Add **s** or **es** to verbs when the noun names one person, place, or thing.

A dog howl**s**.   There is one dog, so add an *s* to the verb.

The dogs howl.   There is more than one dog, so do not change the verb.

Write a noun or verb to complete each sentence.

1. Three bears _____.

2. Leaves _____.

3. A tiger _____.

4. The turtle _____.

5. _____ crunches.

6. A _____ smells.

7. _____ sing.

8. The _____ sleep.

WRITE AWAY

Some nouns name one and more than one. One example is *sheep*. Write a sentence that uses the word to mean more than one sheep.

_____

_____

Statements

Now that you know about sentences, let's take a look at different kinds of sentences. Why do you need to know about them? Using a variety of sentences keeps a reader interested so that he or she will read on. A story that has only one kind of sentence would probably be boring to read.

A **statement** tells something. Like all sentences, it begins with a capital letter. Every statement ends with a **period (.)**. Most sentences that you write are statements.

John eats cheese sandwiches.
The dog raised its paw.

Write a statement using each word below. Don't forget to use the correct beginning and ending.

1. corn _____

2. kick _____

3. brother _____

4. loudly_____

5. scary _____

WRITE AWAY

On another sheet of paper, draw a picture of something. Write five clues about it. The clues should be statements. Read the clues to a friend or family member so that he or she can guess the name of the picture.

Questions

Do you know what a **question** is? A question is another kind of sentence. It asks something. Each question begins with a capital letter and ends with a **question mark (?)**. Some of the words that begin a question include *who, what, where, when, why,* and *how.*

What is your favorite song?

Would you like onions on your pizza?

Why is it important to use questions in your writing? Questions can help you organize your ideas in the prewriting stage. They let you know if you have all the information you need before you begin writing.

Questions also help get readers involved in what you are saying. Readers have to stop and think about the answer. They will want to keep on reading to find out what you have to say about the question. Questions are a good way to use the writing trait of sentence fluency.

Imagine that you are writing about making lunch. Write questions using the words below that you could ask in the prewriting step.

1. Who _____

2. What _____

3. Where _____

4. When _____

5. Why _____

6. How _____

WRITE AWAY

Think of a friend or family member that you would like to know more about. Write five questions on another sheet of paper. Then ask the person the questions. Record the answers as statements.

24

Exclamations

Wow! Now you will learn about **exclamations!** How exciting! Actually, sentences that are exclamations are exciting. They show strong feeling. Like other sentences, exclamations begin with a capital letter. They end with an **exclamation mark (!)**.

What a big fish you caught!

Watch out for that snake!

Stop! You're going too fast!

These weights are really heavy!

Exclamations can help show the writing traits of voice and sentence fluency. When you write, exclamations give the reader a clue that something exciting is happening. It might mean that you are excited about the topic. It can also mean that the action in the story is exciting. Using exclamations will certainly keep the reader reading.

Write an exclamation using each word below. Don't forget to use the correct beginning and ending.

1. terrific _____

2. whale _____

3. catch _____

4. yippee _____

5. taste _____

WRITE AWAY

Imagine that you are at the circus. On another sheet of paper, write five exclamations that you might say while you are watching the show.

Commands

Put your pencil down. Now read this page.

The two sentences above are examples of a **command**. A command is a sentence that gives an order or a direction. A command begins with a capital letter and ends with a **period (.)**. At first glance, the sentence looks like it does not have a subject. But there is one— it's you. When a command is given, the listener knows that he or she is the one that has to do the action. It is understood that the listener is the subject of the sentence.

You probably won't use too many commands in the works that you write. Yet there will be times when commands are useful. For example, if you want to tell a reader how to make something, you will use command sentences. You will use commands to give directions, too.

Imagine that a friend is visiting your house. Write directions from the front door to your bedroom.

_____

_____

_____

_____

WRITE AWAY

Choose something to hide, such as a toy. On another sheet of paper, write directions to tell how to find it. Give the directions to a friend or family member and ask him or her to find the object. If you wrote clear directions, he or she should find it easily!

Quotations and Dialogue

Do you ever repeat words that a friend or family member has told you? If so, you are saying a **quote,** or the exact words that he or she said. The sentence with a quote is a **quotation**.

Here is a quotation.

Ben Franklin said, "Early to bed and early to rise makes a man healthy, wealthy, and wise."

In quotations, you write **quotation marks (" ")** before and after the exact words a speaker says. The first word a speaker says also begins with a capital letter. Use a **comma (,)** to separate the speaker's name from the quotation.

You might also see quotation marks in a story that you are reading. In this kind of sentence, a **character** is speaking. A character is the real or made-up human or animal in a story. When characters speak together, you are reading **dialogue**. Like a quotation, dialogue uses quotation marks and a comma.

Talk with a friend or family member. Write three examples of quotations or dialogue that you hear or say.

_____

_____

_____

_____

WRITE AWAY

Who is your favorite story character? Imagine that the character is visiting you today. On another sheet of paper, write a dialogue the two of you might have.

Notice Nouns

Writing takes time and practice. There are many skills that you can learn to make your work interesting and fun to read. You already learned about different kinds of sentences. You found out that using different kinds of sentences adds variety to your writing. People won't be bored, and they will keep reading.

Now let's take a look at other writing skills. These skills not only keep the reader interested, but they make the writing clearer.

Read this sentence: **She** walked to the **park**.

It is a plain, boring sentence. Would you like to read a story filled with this kind of sentence? Most readers would not! So let's focus on how to jazz it up using the writing trait of word choice. Here are some ways to change the sentence. Notice the **nouns.**

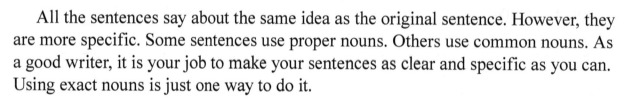

Maya walked to **Oak Hill Park**.
The **woman** walked to the **picnic area**.
A **girl** walked to the **soccer field**.
The **child** walked to the **playground**.

All the sentences say about the same idea as the original sentence. However, they are more specific. Some sentences use proper nouns. Others use common nouns. As a good writer, it is your job to make your sentences as clear and specific as you can. Using exact nouns is just one way to do it.

Rewrite each sentence. Replace each noun or pronoun with specific nouns.

1. The dog barked at the cat. _____

2. The girl called to her. _____

3. We swam in the water. _____

WRITE AWAY

Look around you. What is happening? On another sheet of paper, write four sentences that tell what you see. Use nouns that give specific and clear details.

28

Very Vibrant Verbs

Like nouns, **verbs** can add interest and variety to your writing. Remember that a verb is the word in the sentence that shows action or a state of being. It is important to choose the right verb to give a clear picture of what is happening in your writing.

Look at the verb in this sentence.

The squirrels **ran** up the tree.

The verb *ran* does not give much detail. Here are some other verbs that you could use. These verbs are more lively, or vibrant. They make the sentence more interesting.

The squirrels **scampered** up the tree.
The squirrels **scurried** up the tree.
The squirrels **raced** up the tree.
The squirrels **dashed** up the tree.

Using vibrant verbs will help a reader enjoy your work.

Rewrite each sentence. Replace each verb with a more vibrant word.

1. The bird flew in the sky.

   _____

2. The wind blew the trees.

   _____

3. Ellen laughed at the joke.

   _____

WRITE AWAY

Look around you. What is happening? On another sheet of paper, write four sentences that tell about the action. Use vibrant verbs in the sentences.

29

Verb Clues

Choosing vibrant **verbs** can make your work more interesting. Verbs have another role, too. They can add the writing trait of voice to your work. They can give readers clues about how story characters feel.

Read this sentence: Marta **went** to the bakery.

The sentence tells what Marta did. But does it tell anything about Marta? No! Let's look at how changing the verb can help you learn more about the character.

- Marta **crept** to the bakery. *Crept* means "moved slowly and quietly." Using this verb shows that Marta is scared. She moved slowly so she could look around her.
- Marta **rushed** to the bakery. *Rushed* means "hurried." Using this verb shows that Marta is moving with speed.
- Marta **skipped** to the bakery. *Skipped* means "hopped from one foot to the other." Using this verb shows that Marta is happy.

When you write, try to choose verbs that give clues. Then you won't have to write as many details. It is also fun for your readers to figure out the clues to learn more.

Read the sentence below. Then answer the questions. Rewrite the sentence with a different verb to show each clue.

Paulo ate the sandwich.

1. How could you say that Paulo was very hungry when he ate?

_____

2. How could you say that Paulo was not very hungry when he ate?

_____

WRITE AWAY

Said is a verb used in dialogue: *"I'm home," Al said.* Think of five verbs to replace *said*. Rewrite the sentence using those verbs on another sheet of paper.

Active and Passive Voice Verbs

There is one more detail about verbs that you should know. It is how to write using an **active voice**. In a sentence with an active voice, the subject does the action.

Read these two sentences.
- Anna flies a kite.
- The kite was flown by Anna.

The first sentence is written in the active voice. Anna, the subject of the sentence, is the one who flies the kite. However, the second sentence is in **passive voice**. The subject, the kite, does not do the action. All passive voice sentences use two verbs. One of the verbs is a **helping verb**. The helping verbs are *am, is, are, was, were, be,* and *been*. The other verb is a main verb.

Sometimes you may use a helping verb in a sentence, but it is still active.

Anna was flying a kite.

In this sentence, **Anna** is the subject, and she is doing the action.

The sentences below are written in passive voice. Rewrite each sentence so it is in active voice.

1. The songs were sung by children.

_____

2. The food has been eaten by us.

_____

WRITE AWAY

On another sheet of paper, write four sentences that use active voice verbs. Then rewrite them using passive voice verbs. Discuss with a friend or family member how you know the sentences are passive or active.

Adding Details with Adjectives

Imagine that you took a trip to a farm. You enjoyed the trip so much that after your trip, you decided to write a description of what you saw. You wrote:

A cow was in the field. A peacock spread its tail. The horses ran.

Is there something wrong with your description? Yes, you're missing **adjectives!** Adjectives are those wonderful words that describe nouns. They tell how many, what color, or what size and shape something is. They also tell how something feels, tastes, smells, or sounds. Adding adjectives to a sentence adds interest and detail. Using these words also gives the reader a more exact picture.

So let's try describing the farm again.

A **large brown** and **white** cow grazed in the **tall green** grass. A **bright blue** peacock fanned its tail, showing its **beautiful green, gold,** and **purple** feathers. The **valiant brown** horses galloped across the **wide open** field.

This description is much better! Adjectives can really add sparkle to any writing.

Rewrite the sentences. Include at least three adjectives in each sentence.

1. Frogs jump in the water.

   _____

2. The boys ride their bikes.

   _____

3. Clouds float in the sky.

   _____

WRITE AWAY

Think about a soccer ball. Write at least four sentences that describe it on another sheet of paper. See how many adjectives you can use.

Name _____ Date _____

The Reader's Senses

Think about spending a day at the beach. You would use all five of your **senses** to enjoy the day. You would see the blue ocean. You would hear the waves crashing on the shore. You would feel the hot, grainy sand under your feet. You would smell the salt in the air and taste it when you swim.

If you wrote a letter to a friend, what would you say about the beach? Writing good details is a special skill. You would want to make your friend see, smell, taste, hear, and feel everything. To be a good writer, you choose words that relate to the reader's senses. You can use adjectives to describe the senses you experience.

Here are some sense words.

sight: red, round, little
smell: rotten, sweet, smoky
taste: sweet, bitter, chocolate
hearing: loud, soft, crunchy
touch: smooth, rough, hot

Choose adjectives carefully. Make the reader feel that he or she is "there."

Choose adjectives that you could use to describe each object. Write the adjectives on the line.

1. a strawberry _____

2. a snowball _____

3. a fish _____

4. a song _____

WRITE AWAY

What is your favorite food? On another sheet of paper, write a sentence that uses each sense to describe it.

33

Words That Paint a Picture

It is important to help a reader understand an idea. Choosing the right words can help you do this. You can use words to help you paint a picture. Sometimes writers compare two things that are alike. Comparing two things helps a reader better understand what he or she is reading in a more exciting way.

His socks smelled **like rotten eggs**.

The room was **as hot as an oven**.

Read each word picture. Underline the two things that are being compared. Then tell how they are alike.

1. The fog covered the top of the hill like a blanket.

   _____

2. Like an umbrella, the tree protected us from the rain.

   _____

3. The boat cut through the water like a knife through butter.

   _____

4. The moon smiled down on us just as Grandma always did.

   _____

WRITE AWAY

Read the sentences below. Rewrite each to help paint pictures.

The waves hit the beach. _____

_____

The children played. _____

_____

Adding Details with Adverbs

Like adjectives, **adverbs** add interest to any sentence. Adverbs describe verbs, adjectives, or other adverbs. Most adverbs tell when, where, or how. Many adverbs end in *ly*. You can add adverbs to any writing to give more details.

Grandma is coming. She will arrive at the airport. We will pick her up.

Now let's add some adverbs to make these sentences clearer.

Grandma is coming **here** (where). She will arrive at the airport **tomorrow** (when). We will **happily** (how) pick her up.

Rewrite the sentences. Include an adverb in each sentence.

1. The camel walks.

_____

2. The campers will set up a tent.

_____

3. It is time to leave the beach.

_____

WRITE AWAY

Write adverbs that fit each group.

tell when: _____

tell where: _____

tell how: _____

Synonyms

You have been learning how the words you choose can make your writing clear. They can help a reader see, hear, smell, taste, and touch the things you are describing. Words can also help your reader feel a certain way.

Word choice is important in another way. Sometimes you have to name the same item several times in your sentences. You can use **synonyms** to make your writing more interesting. A synonym is a word that almost has the same meaning as another word.

These words are synonyms: *pretty   beautiful   lovely   gorgeous*

Do these words mean the same thing? No, but they all tell how nice something looks. A thesaurus is a book that can help you find synonyms. But you have to be sure that the meaning of the word is as similar as possible.

Write a synonym for the underlined word in each sentence.

1. Sam decided to climb a big tree.

   Synonym: _____

2. He started to climb up into its branches.

   Synonym: _____

3. He discovered a beehive in the tree.

   Synonym: _____

4. Sam decided to pick another tree to climb.

   Synonym: _____

WRITE AWAY

On another sheet of paper, write five words. Then write as many synonyms as you can for each of your words.

Antonyms

An **antonym** is a word that means the opposite of another word.

These word pairs are antonyms: *big/little   fast/slow   tall/short*

When describing something, you can help a reader get a clearer picture if you use antonyms in your sentence. The words help the reader tell how two things are different.

The **bright** star twinkled in the **dark** sky.

The **loud** squawk of the parrot broke the **quiet** morning.

Write an antonym for the underlined word to complete each sentence.

1. Jill pulled the <u>little</u> weeds from between the _____ flowers.

2. It was <u>hard</u> work, so Jill decided to make the work _____.

3. She watered the <u>dry</u> soil to make it _____.

4. Jill had worked <u>slowly</u> at first. Now she could work very _____.

WRITE AWAY

Write five antonym pairs not listed on this page. Then write sentences using the words.

_____

_____

_____

_____

_____

_____

_____

37

Homophones

You are learning how important it is to choose the best words for your work. It is just as important to spell the words correctly. Most of the time, you can look up a word in a dictionary to find its spelling. However, some words have spellings that are confusing. These words are **homophones**. They sound alike, but they have different spellings and meanings.

Read these sentences. Which is correct?
- Be sure to write each word right on the paper.
- Be sure to right each word write on the paper.

Write and *right* are homophones. The correct sentence is, *Be sure to write each word right on the paper.* It is important when you proofread your work to look for homophones. You can use editing marks to show how to correct the mistakes.

Be sure to ∧~~right~~ each word ∧~~write~~ on the paper.

         write   *right*

Use the Proofreading Marks on page 115 to correct the homophone mistakes.

1. Their was won weak left before the big race.

2. Vida could knot weight four the day two come.

3. She had practiced sew hard.

4. Vida new that she wood be the won to win the race!

WRITE AWAY

On another sheet of paper, write five homophone pairs not listed on this page. Write sentences that use both words in each pair.

Joining Sentences with the Same Subject

You know how to keep a reader's interest by choosing lively and specific words. You can also choose sense words or words that paint a picture. Now it is time to think about how the whole sentence can help make writing more interesting.

Many short sentences can be boring for a reader. They do not flow smoothly, and they sound choppy. To help improve sentence fluency, you can join sentences that have the same subject.

Read these sentences.

Jan was hungry. **Jan** was thirsty.

Jan was hungry and thirsty.

To combine sentences with the same subject, follow these steps.
- Look for short sentences that have the same subject.
- Write the subject.
- Write the predicates. Use the conjunction *and* between the predicates.

Combine each pair of sentences. Write one sentence.

1. The chicken danced. The chicken sang.

   _____

2. The barnyard animals stood up. The barnyard animals clapped.

   _____

3. The chicken decided to put on a show. The chicken decided to travel around the world.

   _____

WRITE AWAY

Continue the story of the singing chicken. On another sheet of paper, write sentences that tell what happens to the chicken. Look for sentences that you can combine. Tell a friend or family member how you could combine short sentences.

Joining Sentences with the Same Predicate

Just like joining sentences that have the same subject, you can also join sentences that have the same predicate. The sentences will flow more smoothly and have better rhythm.

Read these sentences.

Fruits **grow in the garden**. Vegetables **grow in the garden**.
Fruits and vegetables grow in the garden.

To combine sentences with the same predicate, follow these steps.
- Look for short sentences that have the same predicate.
- Write the subjects. Use the conjunction *and* between the subjects.
- Write the predicate.

Combine each pair of sentences. Write one sentence.

1. The moon lit up the night sky. The stars lit up the night sky.

_____

2. Some crickets sang. Some birds sang.

_____

3. Neisha smiled at the sounds. Laura smiled at the sounds.

_____

WRITE AWAY

Continue the story about Neisha and Laura. On another sheet of paper, write sentences that tell something the girls do. Look for sentences that you can combine. Tell a friend or family member how you could combine short sentences.

Joining Sentences with the Same Idea

When you write several sentences together, they often share an idea. There is a way to make them more interesting. Join short, choppy sentences together.

Read these sentences.

    Rick has a pet dog. Jean has a pet cat.
      (Shared idea: pets)
    Rick has a pet dog, but Jean has a pet cat.

    Abe can go swimming. He can go to a movie.
      (Shared idea: Abe)
    Abe can go swimming, or he can go to a movie.

    The children want a snack. They want a drink.
      (Shared idea: children)
    The children want a snack, and they want a drink.

To combine sentences, follow these steps.

- Look for short sentences that tell about the same idea.
- Use the conjunctions *or, but,* or *and* to join the sentences. *And* shows an addition, *but* shows a difference, and *or* shows a choice.
- Write a **comma (,)** before the conjunction.

Combine each pair of sentences. Write one sentence.

1. Ray heard a noise. He did not know where it came from.

_____

_____

2. The noise could have come from under his bed. It could have come from his closet.

_____

_____

3. Ray opened his closet. He looked inside.

_____

Joining Sentences to List Words in a Series

A **series** is a list of three or more words or items. Short, choppy sentences can be combined into one long, clear sentence with a series.

Read these sentences.

Mary can buy a pencil. Mary can buy a pen or some crayons.

Mary can buy a pencil, a pen, or some crayons.

Fish are swimming in the pond. Frogs are swimming in the pond. Turtles are swimming in the pond.

Fish, frogs, and turtles are swimming in the pond.

To combine sentences, follow these steps.

- Look for two or three short sentences that tell about the same idea.
- Use the conjunctions *or* or *and* to join the sentences. *And* shows an addition, and *or* shows a choice.
- Write a **comma (,)** to separate items.

Combine each set of sentences. Write one sentence.

1. The fall leaves are red. The fall leaves are orange. The fall leaves are yellow.

   _____

2. Jan rakes the leaves. Mother and Dad rake the leaves.

   _____

3. Ken can rake the leaves. Ken can bag or mulch the leaves.

   _____

WRITE AWAY

What will you eat for dinner? Write two sentences that contain a series of three or more words or items. Use another sheet of paper. Use the word *or* in one sentence. Use the word *and* in the other sentence.

Name _____ Date _____

Sentence Length

Remember that sentence fluency is when the sentences in your writing flow smoothly and have a rhythm. You can achieve this by writing long and short sentences.

Read these sentences.

Captain Garza entered the space rocket. He closed the door. He sat in his chair. He began to push some buttons. The engine roared. Soon he would blast off.

All the sentences are short and choppy, so the text is not much fun to read. You can join some sentences to make them longer. Other sentences can be left short. Changing the sentence length can make the text flow more smoothly.

Here are two examples of how to change the sentence fluency.

Captain Garza entered the space rocket. He closed the door, sat in his chair, and began to push some buttons. The engine roared. Soon he would blast off.

Captain Garza entered the space rocket and closed the door. He sat in his chair. He began to push some buttons so that the engine roared. Soon he would blast off.

Rewrite the text below so that some of the sentence lengths change.

Willie Wasp had a nest by the pool. It was a nice shady spot. Willie had so much to do. He could go swimming. He could sleep. He could fly to see his friends.

_____

_____

_____

_____

WRITE AWAY

On another sheet of paper, show a different way to write the text above. Read both examples to a friend or family member. Ask the friend or family member to tell which one he or she likes better and why.

Sentence Variety

Remember that in order to have sentence fluency, our sentences need to flow smoothly and have a rhythm. One way to help improve fluency is to vary your sentence beginnings.

Read this paragraph.

Mr. Patel stretched his arms. Mr. Patel slowly got out of bed. Mr. Patel walked to his closet. Mr. Patel grabbed his clothes, got dressed, and was ready to go eat breakfast.

All of the sentences in this paragraph begin the same way—with Mr. Patel. The sentences are boring and difficult to read. By varying the sentence beginnings, the paragraph will become livelier and easier to read. Read the new paragraph below. Notice how the sentences have changed.

On Friday morning, Mr. Patel stretched his arms and slowly got out of bed. He walked to the closet. After grabbing his clothes and getting dressed, he was ready to go eat breakfast.

Rewrite the text below so that some of the sentence beginnings change.

Sal hated to write. Sal didn't know how to put his thoughts into words. Sal kept writing in his journal, though. Sal began to notice that his writing was slowly improving.

_____

_____

_____

_____

WRITE AWAY

On another sheet of paper, show a different way to write the text above. Read both examples to a friend or family member. Ask the friend or family member which one he or she likes better and why.

Run-on Sentences

A **run-on sentence** tells about more than one main idea. It is hard to understand because the punctuation is not correct.

Here is an example of a run-on sentence.
We started early we still arrived late.

You can fix a run-on sentence two ways.
- Join the two sentences with a comma and a conjunction.
  We started early, **but** we still arrived late.

- Write the run-on sentence as two separate sentences.
  We started early. **We** still arrived late.

Correct each run-on sentence. Write the new sentence or sentences on the line.

1. Pat got out a glass she filled it with water.

_____

2. Pat tapped the glass with a spoon she liked the sound.

_____

3. She drank some of the water Pat tapped the glass again.

_____

4. Pat filled glasses with different amounts of water then she played a tune.

_____

WRITE AWAY

Here is a very long run-on sentence. How would you fix it? Write the new sentences on another sheet of paper.

Leslie could not find her small black kitten she looked in every room including her bedroom and the kitchen she finally found the kitten asleep in the laundry basket.

Proofreading Sentences

You have learned a lot about sentences. You have practiced making sentences better, too. Now it is time for you to learn how to proofread them using special marks!

Look at the Proofreading Marks on page 115. You can use these marks when you edit to show how to correct your mistakes. You use them to show where to add commas and periods. You use them to show where to write capital letters or lowercase letters.

Here is an example of how to edit a sentence.

Jack and jill went up a hill.

Correct each sentence using proofreading marks.

1. Dr tooth is my dentist

2. I went to visit her on tuesday

3. She clened my teeth she flossed my teeth

4. when was the last time that you went too the Dentist

WRITE AWAY

How can proofreading marks make writing a clean copy easier? Write several sentences that explain your ideas. Discuss your ideas with a friend or family member.

_____

_____

_____

_____

_____

46

Self-Assessment: Sentences

You should feel very comfortable with writing sentences now. So it's time to use these skills in the writing process. Just follow the steps below.

Prewriting

1. What do you like to do? List three activities.

_____

_____

_____

2. Which activity do you feel the strongest about? Circle it.

3. List three details about the activity that a reader would like to know.

_____

_____

_____

Drafting

Write sentences about your favorite activity. Use your ideas from prewriting. Don't worry about making mistakes! Just get the sentences on paper.

_____

_____

_____

_____

_____

_____

Self-Assessment: Sentences, continued

Revising

Look at the sentences you wrote in your draft. How can you make them better? Do they all make sense? Is your purpose clear? Can you add more details? Can you make your sentences more lively? Can you change the length or pattern of the sentences? Rewrite your sentences to make them better.

_____

_____

_____

_____

_____

_____

_____

Proofreading

You need to look carefully at the sentences you wrote for mistakes. You should read your work once for capital letters. You should read it a second time for end marks and commas. You should read it a third time for spelling. Use the Proofreading Marks on page 115 to show where your mistakes are. You can use the Proofreading Checklist on page 114 as a guide.

Publishing

Now it is time to make a clean copy of your sentences. You can handwrite them on another sheet of paper, or you can type them on the computer. Don't forget to add a title! You might even want to draw a picture of yourself doing the activity. Once your sentences are done, share them with a friend or family member.

Congratulations! You wrote great sentences. As you can see, using the writing process makes writing easy and fun!

What Is a Paragraph?

You know how to write great sentences. Now it's time to learn how to put the sentences together to share your ideas. A **paragraph** is a group of sentences. All the sentences in a paragraph tell about one main idea. The first line of each paragraph is **indented**. This means that the first word is moved to the right slightly. Many paragraphs are about five sentences long.

Here is an example of a paragraph.

A frog can live on land or in water. It has strong and long back legs that help it jump on land. These same legs help it swim quickly in water. Some animals like to eat frogs. The frog can jump into the water to get away from land animals. It can climb up on land to escape water animals. It is a good thing that frogs can live in both places.

Answer the questions. Use the example paragraph above.

1. What is the main idea of the paragraph?

   _____

   _____

2. What are two details that tell about the main idea?

   _____

   _____

   _____

WRITE AWAY

Look in a book. Read one paragraph. On another sheet of paper, tell how you know that it is a paragraph. Discuss your answer with a friend or family member.

Parts of a Paragraph

A paragraph is a group of sentences that tells about one main idea. A paragraph has three parts.

- a **topic sentence**
- **detail sentences**
- a **concluding sentence**

The topic sentence tells the main idea of the paragraph. It is often the first sentence in a paragraph. The detail sentences tell more about the main idea. The concluding sentence is at the end of the paragraph. It uses different words to tell about the main idea. It can also summarize the information in the paragraph.

Read the paragraph below. Then follow the directions.

Hot chocolate is a great drink to have on a cold, dark day. The hot cup warms my hands. The rising steam warms my face. When I drink it, the hot chocolate warms me on the inside from my head to my toes. But the best part is the melted marshmallow. The white goo sticks to the top of my nose and lip. It looks like I have a marshmallow mustache. It makes me laugh. The hot chocolate makes the day a little brighter.

1. Underline the topic sentence.

2. Number the detail sentences.

3. Circle the concluding sentence.

WRITE AWAY

Is the paragraph above a good paragraph? Why or why not?

_____

_____

_____

50

Paragraph Order

Writing follows a certain order: prewriting, drafting, revising, proofreading, and publishing. Paragraphs have a certain order, too.

The first sentence is usually the **topic sentence**. The topic sentence should get the reader's attention. It names the topic, or main idea, of the paragraph, but it does not give exact details.

The other sentences are the **detail sentences**. They form the body of the paragraph. They give details about the topic.

The last sentence is the **concluding sentence**. It tells about the main idea again, but it uses different words. It can also summarize the information in the paragraph.

Write *1* through *5* to show the best order of the sentences in the paragraph.

_____ She made a peanut butter sandwich.

_____ She went to the kitchen.

_____ Masie was hungry.

_____ She wasn't hungry anymore, but now she was thirsty.

_____ Masie ate the sandwich quickly.

WRITE AWAY

On another sheet of paper, continue the story of Masie. What does she do next? Make sure that you write all the parts of a paragraph and follow the correct paragraph order.

Writing a Topic Sentence

A **topic sentence** tells the main idea of a paragraph. It tells what all the other sentences in the paragraph are about. The topic sentence is usually the first sentence in a paragraph.

A paragraph is about five sentences long. A topic sentence should be narrow enough so that you can write three or four detail sentences that give enough information to clearly tell about the topic. For example, you might want to write about dogs. That is a large topic, and you should narrow it. You should focus on one part about dogs. Choose a topic that you can fully explain in three or four sentences. You could write about how dogs grow. You could write about a job they do, like herd animals or help people. You could even write about how to train a dog.

Topic: dogs   Focus: guide dogs

Topic sentence: Some dogs help people who cannot see.

Read each topic below. Then choose a focus for each topic. Write a topic sentence that you could use to write a paragraph about your topic.

1. Topic: flowers

   Focus: _____

   Topic sentence: _____

2. Topic: paint

   Focus: _____

   Topic sentence: _____

3. Topic: bikes

   Focus: _____

   Topic sentence: _____

WRITE AWAY

On another sheet of paper, write a paragraph using one of your topic sentences.

Writing Detail Sentences

The **detail sentences** make up the body of the paragraph. Detail sentences give specific information about the topic. Detail sentences can give facts or examples. Their main purpose is to help the reader learn more about the topic.

When you write detail sentences, you should choose the most interesting details. The details should also give clear examples to help the reader understand the main idea. First, list all the details you can think of. Then choose the three to five details that best tell about the topic sentence. Write them in an order that makes sense. The sentences should flow smoothly and have rhythm, too.

Think about the topic of guide dogs. Here are some detail sentences.

Some dogs help people who cannot see. **These dogs are called guide dogs. The dogs are trained to keep their person safe. They help their person walk from one place to another and guide their person around objects. Guide dogs even tell their person when someone comes near.**

Read the topic sentence. Follow the directions.

Topic sentence: Spaghetti is a messy food to eat.

1. Write three details about spaghetti. Then circle the two best details.

   _____

   _____

   _____

2. Write two detail sentences that tell about the topic sentence.

   _____

   _____

   _____

WRITE AWAY

On another sheet of paper, write a paragraph using the topic sentence and the detail sentences about spaghetti. Make sure that the sentence order makes sense and that the sentences flow smoothly.

© Houghton Mifflin Harcourt Publishing Company

Writing a Concluding Sentence

A **concluding sentence** ends the paragraph. It usually restates the topic sentence using different words. The concluding sentence sums up the information in the paragraph. It can also explain what the information means.

Think of your paragraph as a sandwich. The two slices of bread hold all the details inside—the peanut butter, the jelly, the pickle slices. The top slice of bread is the topic sentence. The bottom slice of bread is the concluding sentence. It is almost like the top slice but not exactly, just as the concluding sentence is like the topic sentence but not exactly. Read the paragraph about guide dogs. Notice the topic sentence and the concluding sentence.

Some dogs help people who cannot see. These dogs are called guide dogs. The dogs are trained to keep their person safe. They help their person walk from one place to another and guide their person around objects. Guide dogs even tell their person when someone comes near. **The dogs and their person are partners.**

Read the paragraph below. Then write possible concluding sentences for the paragraph. Be sure your concluding sentences restate the main idea in different words. One possible concluding sentence is done for you.

Have you ever heard someone say, "It's easy as pie"? It means that the activity you are doing is easy. The saying started long ago. Someone compared the activity to eating a sweet and tasty piece of pie. The person was right, too.

Concluding sentence 1: _Eating pie is easy—especially if it is apple!_ _____

_____

Concluding sentence 2: _____

_____

Concluding sentence 3: _____

_____

Keeping to the Topic

When you write a paragraph, all the sentences must tell about the **main idea**. The main idea is the same as the topic. All the details in the paragraph must tell about the topic. If a sentence does not keep to the topic, you should take it out of the paragraph.

Suppose you're writing a paragraph telling how an ant carried a crumb off a picnic table. Would you include a detail sentence describing an ant nest? No! While all the sentences talk about an ant, the focus of the paragraph is about an ant carrying a crumb. The sentence about the ant nest would need to be removed.

Read the underlined topic sentence. Choose detail sentences that keep to the topic. Write a paragraph using the topic sentence and the detail sentences you chose. Use another sheet of paper if necessary.

The Fourth of July is a fun holiday.

And best of all, fireworks light up the night sky!

Family and friends get together.

Dogs swim in the lake.

Many towns have parades.

They have picnics in the park.

People display the United States flag.

_____

_____

_____

_____

_____

_____

_____

Transition Words

Think back to what you learned about sentence fluency. Sentence fluency is when the text flows smoothly and has rhythm. Some words you choose can also help the flow of text in a paragraph.

Read these paragraphs.

There was a young girl who lived with her stepmother and two stepsisters. They did not treat her well. She had to do all the work. The prince of her land had a ball. She didn't have anything to wear. She could not go. Her godmother gave her a beautiful gown to wear. She went to the ball and danced with the prince.

Once there was a young girl who lived with her stepmother and two stepsisters. Even though she did all the work, they did not treat her well. One day, the prince of her land had a ball. Since she didn't have anything to wear, she could not go. However, her godmother gave her a beautiful gown to wear. At last, she went to the ball and danced with the prince.

Which paragraph flows more smoothly? The second one! This paragraph uses the **transition words** *once, even though, one day, since, however,* and *at last* to help move from one idea to the next. Notice that the sentences flow more smoothly in the second paragraph and are not as choppy as in the first paragraph.

Read the paragraph. Using proofreading marks, add the transition words *also* and *sometimes* to make it flow smoothly.

Watermelon is a great fruit to eat on a hot summer day. The sweet flavor bursts

on my tongue. The juice drips down my chin. It falls on my clothes. I get several

seeds in my mouth. You better watch out! I can spit them really far!

Time-Order Words

Think about something that happened to you. How would you tell someone about it? You would tell everything that happened in the order it happened. You would start at the beginning, explain the events in the middle, and tell how it ended. **Time-order words** are transition words that tell exactly when something happens.

Here are some time-order words.

before	after	first	next	then	finally
during	later	soon	when	second	as soon as

Like storytellers, writers use time-order words. The words help tell sequence.

Here is a paragraph that uses time-order words.

Kendra wanted to sell lemonade. **First,** she made the lemonade. **Then,** she put it in a thermos. **Next,** Kendra got some cups. **Soon,** she was ready. Kendra put everything in her wagon. **Finally,** she pulled her wagon along the sidewalk. The neighbors working in the yard were happy to buy Kendra's lemonade on such a hot day.

Number the sentences in the order the events happen. The topic sentence is numbered for you. Then write the sentences in paragraph form. Use another sheet of paper. Remember to indent the first sentence.

_____1_____ Making pizza is easy.

_____ Finally, you bake it.

_____ Then, you spread tomato sauce on the crust.

_____ However, the easiest part is eating the pizza!

_____ Next, you add your favorite toppings, like cheese and tomatoes.

_____ First, you spread out the dough to make the crust.

Audience

People write because they have something to say. They often want to share their writing with others. The people who read the work are the **audience**. You have to think about your audience before you write. The audience can affect what you will write and how.

Here are some questions that can help you think about your audience.

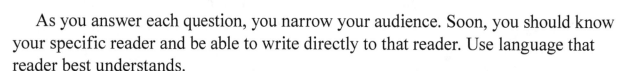

- Who will read my writing?
- Who will be most interested in this topic?
- Am I trying to get someone to think as I do?
- Do I like my audience? Do I want them to like me?
- Will I write for younger children or for adults?
- Will I write for people my own age?
- What might the audience already know about this topic?
- What words will this audience understand?

As you answer each question, you narrow your audience. Soon, you should know your specific reader and be able to write directly to that reader. Use language that reader best understands.

Read each topic. Choose a word from the box to tell who might be the audience. Some topics can have more than one audience.

myself	family members	people in the community
teenagers	children	friends
		adults

1. an entry in my journal _____

2. a news article about a cleanup day at the park _____

3. a story about snowboarding _____

4. a story about singing mice _____

5. a letter telling about my birthday party _____

Voice

You learned about **voice** in Unit 1. Voice is showing how you feel in your writing. The words you choose and the sentences you write are the way you show voice. When you use the trait of voice, you are able to make the reader feel the way you do through your writing.

Read these sentences.

Singing a song, I skipped along the sidewalk.
Glaring at a man, I stomped down the sidewalk.

People sing and skip when they are happy. Clearly the first sentence shows a happy voice. In the second sentence, the words *glaring* and *stomped* show an angry voice.

Another part of voice is to choose words that your audience can understand. You can choose longer and harder words to describe things to older people. Young children would not understand these same words. For example, you could tell your mother that you are feeling cheerful. However, do you think that a four-year-old child would understand the word *cheerful?* Probably not! It would be better to tell the child that you are happy.

Think of something funny that happened to you. Write two paragraphs telling about the same event. The first paragraph should be written for an older audience. The second should be written for a younger audience. Remember to choose words that show the feeling and can be understood by each group. Use another sheet of paper if you need to.

_____

_____

_____

_____

_____

_____

59

Writing Pattern: Main Idea and Details

Proofreading

There are six **writing patterns** that can help you organize your work. You should choose the pattern that will help the reader best understand the topic.

- Main idea and details

- Sequence of events (order of events)

- Compare and contrast (alike and different)

- Problem and solution

- Cause and effect

- Summary

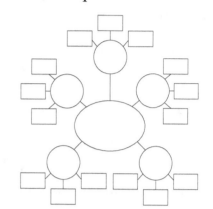

You already know about **main idea** and **details**. The main idea is the most important idea. The details tell more about the main idea. Some details can give a give a clear picture of the main idea. You might choose to describe something using your senses. You might give reasons why you think the way you do, too. When you choose the **main idea and details writing pattern**, a Main Idea and Details Web can help you plan your work.

Look at your shoes. Suppose you have to describe them. Use the Main Idea and Details Web on page 118 to write details about your shoes. Follow the directions below to complete the web.

1. What is the main idea? Write it in the center oval.

2. What senses can you use to describe your shoes? What do they look like? What do they smell like? How do they feel if you touch them? Write one detail in each circle. Draw more circles around the web if you need to.

3. What are some words that describe each detail? Write specific adjectives, adverbs, and nouns that you could use in a paragraph.

WRITE AWAY

On another sheet of paper, write a paragraph that describes your shoes. Follow the steps in the writing process.

Writing Pattern: Sequence of Events

There will probably be a time when you will have to write about an event or tell how to do something. You will need to tell the **sequence** of the actions or steps in order. Think about baking a cake. It would be hard to ice a cake if the directions didn't tell you to bake it first!

In both kinds of writing, you would choose a **sequence of events writing pattern**. When you choose this pattern, a Sequence Chart can help you plan your work. It helps you think about each step. You can plan which time-order clue words to use. Some time-order words are *first, next, then,* and *finally.*

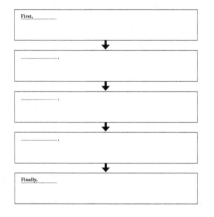

Tell how to make a fruit salad. Use the Sequence Chart on page 119 to write the steps in order. Follow the directions below to complete the chart.

1. What step do you do first? Write it in the top box.

2. What step do you do last? Write it in the bottom box.

3. What steps do you do in between? Write time-order words on the lines. Then write the steps. Draw more boxes if you need to.

WRITE AWAY

On another sheet of paper, write a paragraph that tells how to make a fruit salad. Follow the steps in the writing process.

Writing Pattern: Compare and Contrast

When you **compare**, you tell how two or more things are alike. When you **contrast**, you tell how they are different. For example, to compare your bedroom to that of another family member, you could say that both rooms have a bed and a closet. To contrast them, you could say that your bedroom is neatly picked up, but the family member's bedroom has clothes and books all over the floor.

The **compare and contrast writing pattern** is useful if you want to inform an audience about a topic that is new to them. It will help your audience clearly understand the information. When you choose this pattern, a Venn diagram can help you plan your work.

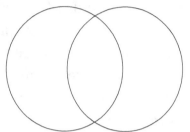

Compare a pen and pencil. Use the Venn diagram on page 120 to list how they are alike and different. Follow the directions below to complete the diagram.

1. Label each circle with a tool name. Write *pencil* above one circle. Write *pen* above the other circle.

2. Look where the circles overlap. Write words that tell how the tools are alike in this space. For example, you might write *writing tool* or *pointed*.

3. In the circle under *pencil*, write words that describe the pencil. They should tell how it is different from the pen. Think about color, shape, and materials it is made of.

4. In the circle under *pen*, write words that describe the pen. They should tell how it is different from the pencil. Think about color, shape, and materials it is made of.

WRITE AWAY

On another sheet of paper, write a paragraph that compares and contrasts a pen and a pencil. Follow the steps in the writing process.

Writing Pattern: Problem and Solution

A **problem** is something that is wrong. It needs to be fixed. A **solution** is the way to fix the problem. A **problem and solution writing pattern** is often useful if you are trying to get the audience to think the way you do. It can also be used if you are explaining something that is a problem.

When you use this pattern, it is important to make sure that the audience understands the problem. You should give examples and details that are clear and specific. You should also tell why the solution works. When you choose this pattern, a Problem and Solution Chart can help you plan your work.

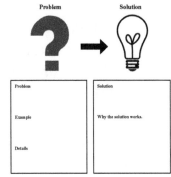

Think about a problem that you had with a friend. Use the Problem and Solution Chart on page 121 to explain the details. Follow the directions below to complete the diagram.

1. Write the problem. Give an example and list two or three details about the problem.

2. Write the solution. Tell why the solution worked.

WRITE AWAY

On another sheet of paper, write a paragraph that tells about the problem that you had with a friend. Explain the solution. Follow the steps in the writing process.

Writing Pattern: Cause and Effect

A **cause** is why something has happened. An **effect** is what happened because of this. For example, imagine that you are eating an ice-cream cone on a hot day. The ice cream is melting faster than you can eat it. In this case, the cause is the heat. The effect is that the ice cream is melting.

The example above is a simple cause and effect event. However, there are times when one cause and effect pair can lead to a chain of cause and effect pairs. Think about the ice cream example above. Suppose dripping ice cream splashes on your toe. An ant comes to eat the ice cream that dripped. The ant bites your toe, which causes you to drop the whole cone. As you can see, each effect leads to another cause. Each cause leads to another effect.

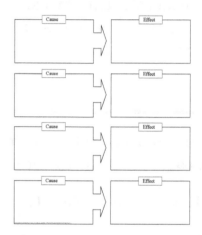

The **cause and effect writing pattern** is useful if you are telling about events that your audience may not know about. You should clearly state the cause and the effect so that a reader can understand why, how, and what in an event. You can use a Cause and Effect Chart to help you plan your work.

Think about a time you got hurt. Use the Cause and Effect Chart on page 122 to explain the details. Follow the directions below to complete the chart.

1. Write the cause. Use exact nouns and verbs to explain the details.

2. Write the effect, or what happened. Use sense words so that the audience can "see" the effect.

WRITE AWAY

On another sheet of paper, write a paragraph that tells about the time that you got hurt. Clearly explain the cause and the effect. Follow the steps in the writing process.

Writing Pattern: Summary

Think about your last trip somewhere. If someone asked you about it, what would you tell the person? Would you describe the clothes you wore? Would you list everything you did? Probably not! You wouldn't want the person to get bored. More than likely you would tell where and when you took the trip and the most important details.

When you tell the most important details of an event, you are **summarizing**. When you summarize, you tell who, what, where, when, why, and how. You might use the **summary writing pattern** if you want to give your audience a short description of something that was very long. Remember that you must give the most important details so the audience understands the event but the readers won't get bored. You can use a Summary Chart to help you plan your work.

Who	Summary
What	
Where	
When	
Why	
How	

Think about your last trip. Use the Summary Chart on page 123 to list the most important details. Follow the directions below to complete the chart.

1. Give the most important details on the left side of the box. Tell who, what, where, when, why, and how. You do not need to write complete sentences.

2. Use the details from the left side of the chart to tell about the trip. Do not include any extra information. Write as few sentences as you can, but be sure to include all the details.

WRITE AWAY

On another sheet of paper, write a paragraph that summarizes your trip. You can include a few more details that you think your audience might like to hear. Don't forget to include a topic and concluding sentence! Follow the steps in the writing process.

Self-Assessment: Paragraphs

> You should understand how to write paragraphs now. So it's time to use these skills in the writing process. Just follow the steps below.

Prewriting

1. What do you know a lot about? List three ideas.

   _____

   _____

   _____

2. Which of the ideas above do you think is the most interesting? Circle it.

3. Who would like to know about this idea? Who could be your audience?

   _____

4. List three details about the idea that your audience would like to know.

   _____

   _____

   _____

5. What is your topic sentence? Remember that it should tell about your main idea.

   _____

   _____

6. What writing pattern will best help your audience understand the topic?

   _____

Self-Assessment: Paragraphs, continued

Drafting

On another sheet of paper, write your topic sentence. Write at least three detail sentences that tell about your topic sentence. Use your ideas from prewriting. Then write a concluding sentence. Don't worry about making mistakes! Just get the sentences on paper.

Revising

Look at the paragraph that you wrote in your draft. How can you make it better? Does it make sense? Is your purpose clear? Can you add more details to some of the sentences? Can you make some words more exact or lively? Can you change the length or pattern of the sentences? Did you use words that your audience can understand? Rewrite your paragraph to make it better.

Proofreading

You need to look carefully at your paragraph to find mistakes. You should read the sentences once for capital letters. You should read them a second time for end marks and commas. You should read them a third time for spelling. You can use the Proofreading Checklist on page 114 as a guide. Use the Proofreading Marks on page 115 to show you where the mistakes are.

Publishing

Now it is time to make a clean copy of your paragraph. You can handwrite it on another sheet of paper or type it on the computer. Don't forget to add a title! You might even want to draw a picture to go along with your paragraph. Once your paragraph is complete, share it with your audience. They're sure to enjoy it!

Personal Narrative

It's time to focus on the different forms of writing. A **personal narrative** is a story telling about something that has happened to the writer. When you write a personal narrative, you are writing about something that has happened to YOU!

You have already written several personal narratives, but here are some hints that will make your stories even better.

- Tell about one event that has happened to you.
- Describe other characters. Use the pronouns *I, me,* and *my.*
- Include a beginning, a middle, and an end.
- The topic sentence should catch the reader's attention.
- The detail sentences should tell about the events in order. Use time-order words such as *first*, *next*, and *finally.*
- The concluding sentence should give a summary of the event.

Here is an example of a personal narrative paragraph.

Today started out all wrong! When I looked at the clock, the numbers showed 7:00. I was going to be late for school. So I bolted out of bed. I put on the first shirt and pants that I saw. Then, I got my backpack. Next, I grabbed a slice of bread and some milk and raced to the bus stop. I waited and waited for the bus. I thought I had missed it. After a while, my friend Keith rode by on his bike. He laughed and said, "It's Saturday. Why are you waiting for the school bus?" I couldn't believe that I thought it was a school day!

Follow the directions below.

1. Think about some things that have happened to you. Write a list of three ideas below.

   _____

   _____

2. Which idea would make an exciting personal narrative that others would enjoy reading? Circle it.

Personal Narrative, continued

Use the Prewriting Survey on pages 108–109 to plan your personal narrative paragraph. Complete the organizer you chose on the survey to help you find more details. Then answer the questions below.

1. Who is telling the story? Who are the characters?

   _____

2. What happened at the beginning of the event?

   _____

3. What topic sentence could you write that would get the attention of your audience?

   _____

4. How did you feel during the event? Write at least three words that you can use to show the voice writing trait.

   _____

5. What happened in the middle of the event?

   _____

   _____

6. What did you or someone else say that is important? Write a quotation.

   _____

7. What happened at the end of the event?

   _____

8. How did you feel at the end of the event?

   _____

WRITE AWAY

You have spent a lot of time thinking about your personal narrative. Did you know that you were prewriting your paragraph? The hardest part is done. Now it's time to start your draft. Use another sheet of paper. Review the hints on page 68. They will help you write a great story. Then follow the rest of the steps in the writing process.

Descriptive Paragraph: Person

In a **descriptive paragraph**, a writer describes a person, place, or thing. A good descriptive paragraph will use each sense to let the reader see, hear, smell, taste, and feel as well.

Writing a description about a person can be especially fun. You will want to look for details that make the person special. The details can focus on how someone looks, sounds, or moves. Then you need to find the same special words to help the reader get to know this person.

Here are some hints that will make your description even better.
- Write a topic sentence about the person to catch the reader's attention.
- Choose words that help readers see, smell, feel, and hear the person.
- Choose lively and interesting adjectives.
- Choose specific verbs that tell how the person moves.
- Include a quotation.

Here is an example of description of a person.

Harry peeked over the fence. He wanted to see who was moving in next door. Harry was surprised to see a face looking back at him. The boy had jet black hair. It was cut short and stood out like spikes from all sides. His big brown eyes sparkled, and his nose was covered in freckles. The boy's voice rang out loudly. "Caught ya' looking!" he laughed. "Ya' wanna' play?" The boy looked to be about his age. Harry smiled back happily and went next door to play.

Follow the directions below.

1. Choose a person you think is interesting or special. Write the name.

_____

2. Write two details that tell how this person is special.

_____

Descriptive Paragraph: Person, continued

Use the Prewriting Survey on pages 108–109 to plan your descriptive paragraph. Complete the organizer you chose on the survey to help you find more details. Then answer the questions below.

1. What is special about the person? Explain.

    _____

2. What are some face or body parts that stand out?

    _____

3. What lively adjectives can you use to describe these parts?

    _____

4. How does the person move?

    _____

5. What are some vivid verbs that you could use to tell about how the person moves?

    _____

6. How does the person talk? Write a quotation.

    _____

7. How does the person smell? Can you compare the smell to another object, like flowers or food?

    _____

8. How does the person make you feel? What words can you use to give voice to the paragraph?

    _____

WRITE AWAY

You have been prewriting ideas for your descriptive paragraph, and now it's time to start your draft. Use another sheet of paper. Review the hints on page 70. Then follow the rest of the steps in the writing process.

Descriptive Paragraph: Place

Just like a description about a person, a description about a place uses words to help readers "feel" they are standing beside the writer. They are seeing, hearing, tasting, smelling, and feeling everything with the writer.

In a place description, you will want to lead the reader through the space. So you want to show the reader how to look.

Here are some hints to make your description even better.

- Tell what a place is like.
- Choose a way to organize the writing to lead the person through it (top to bottom, front to back, side to side, inside to outside, etc.).
- Write a topic sentence that names the place and catches the reader's attention.
- Choose words that help readers see, smell, taste, feel, or hear the place.

Here is an example of a descriptive paragraph about a place.

> Yellowstone National Park has some of the most unique scenery. Great Fountain Geyser sometimes shoots water higher than a twenty-story building. The sparkling water in Yellowstone Lake seems shinier than a mirror. The smell of pine trees fills the air as the many hot springs throw steam into the sky. This park is a diamond in the rough.

Use the Prewriting Survey on pages 108–109 to plan your descriptive paragraph. Complete the organizer you chose on the survey to help you find more details. Then review the hints above. On another sheet of paper, write a draft that describes the place.

Descriptive Paragraph: Place, continued

Look at your draft. Use the questions below to revise your description.

1. Does your topic sentence name the place?

_____

2. How does your topic sentence catch the reader's attention?

_____

3. How did you organize your writing? Did you lead the reader through the place from bottom to top, right to left, or some other way?

_____

4. Does this organization make sense? Why or why not?

_____

5. Name the senses that you have in your writing. Which words did you use to go along with these senses? Is each word the best choice to show that sense?

_____

6. Is there another sense that you can include? What words can you use?

_____

7. Which lively word in your paragraph do you think is the best? Why?

_____

8. What feeling did you want to share with the reader? What words did you use to help the reader feel this way?

_____

WRITE AWAY

The questions above will help you revise your description. Use the suggestions to rewrite a clean copy of your paragraph on another sheet of paper. Then follow the rest of the steps in the writing process.

Descriptive Paragraph: Thing

Remember that a description paints a picture using words. As you write your description about a thing, pretend that the reader is looking over your shoulder. Will your reader understand the thing the same way you do?

When choosing a thing to describe, pick something that will be easy to describe and interesting to read about. You should include enough details so that the reader can clearly understand what you are describing. Yet, there shouldn't be too many details.

Here are some hints to write your description.

- Choose a thing that can be described in three to five sentences.
- Write a topic sentence that names the thing and catches the reader's attention.
- Describe the parts that the audience will want to know more about.
- Choose words that help readers see, smell, taste, feel, or hear the thing.
- Choose specific nouns.
- Choose lively and colorful adjectives.

Here is an example of a descriptive paragraph about a thing.

Beth smiled when her mother placed the big bowl of spaghetti in front of her. The deep red sauce flowed over the long, creamy wheat noodles like lava flowing from a volcano. Big chunks of hamburger floated all around. Beth took a deep breath and smelled the spicy tomatoes. Beth licked her lips.

Use the Prewriting Survey on pages 108–109 to plan your description. Complete the organizer you chose on the survey to help you find more details. Then review the hints above. On another sheet of paper, write a draft that describes the thing.

Descriptive Paragraph, continued

Look at your draft. Use the questions below to revise your description.

1. Will your reader be interested in this thing? Explain. _____

   _____

2. Which parts will your reader want to know more about? Did you describe them?

   _____

3. Name the senses that you have in your writing. Which words did you use to go along
   with these senses? Is each word the best choice to show this sense?

   _____

   _____

4. Read your topic sentence out loud. Does it grab your attention and make you want to
   keep reading? If not, rewrite it to make it more exciting.

   _____

5. Did you use any of these verbs: *is, are, was, were, am, be, been,* or *being*? If so, which

   lively verbs could you write in their place? _____

6. Are all your nouns exact? If not, try to use more specific nouns.

   _____

7. Remember that you can compare two things that are not alike to help a reader
   understand something. What can you compare the thing to?

   _____

8. Do you have short, medium, and long sentences? They will help make the sentences
   flow smoothly.

   _____

WRITE AWAY

The questions above will help you revise your description. Use the suggestions to rewrite a
clean copy of your paragraph on another sheet of paper. Then follow the rest of the steps in
the writing process.

How-to Paragraph

Do you know how to tie your shoe or make your bed? Of course you do! But have you ever thought how you would explain the steps to someone? Think about it for a minute. What materials do you need? How many steps are there?

A **how-to paragraph** tells how to do something in a sequence of steps. It is important to tell each step and in the correct order. It would be silly to tell a person to pull up the blanket if the sheet was not pulled up first.

Here are some hints that will make your how-to paragraph even better.

- Use a topic sentence to state what you will explain.
- Include a detail sentence that tells what materials are needed.
- Give the steps in order using time-order words.
- Take out steps that are not important.
- Write a title that names what you are making.

Here is an example of a how-to paragraph.

How to Make a Sock Puppet

You can make a sock puppet to use in a puppet show. You will need a clean sock, fabric glue, marker, scrap fabric, yarn, and scissors. First, decide what kind of puppet you will make. Then, draw the parts of the face on the scrap fabric and cut out the parts. Next, cut the yarn into pieces. Afterward, glue the face parts and yarn on the foot of the sock. Let the glue dry for several hours. Finally, slide the sock on your hand. You are ready to give a puppet show!

Follow the directions below.

1. Think about some things that you know how to do well. Write a list of three ideas.

_____

_____

_____

2. Which idea do you think a reader would like to learn about? Circle it.

76

How-to Paragraph, continued

Use the Prewriting Survey on pages 108–109 to plan your how-to paragraph. Complete the organizer you chose on the survey to help you find more details. Then answer the questions below.

1. What do you want to tell others to do?

   _____

2. What materials do you need?

   _____

3. In your mind, play a movie of yourself doing the task. List each step on a sequence chart.

4. Will a reader understand each step? If not, how can you make a step clearer?

   _____

5. Which time-order words did you use?

   _____

6. Who will your audience be?

   _____

7. Will the audience understand the words that you use? Why or why not?

   _____

WRITE AWAY

You have planned the steps for how to do something. You have completed most of the prewriting steps. Now it's time to start your draft. Review the hints on page 76. Then draft, revise, proofread, and publish your paper. Use another sheet of paper.

Persuasive Paragraph

A **persuasive paragraph** tries to make the reader do something or think a certain way. For example, the writer may want the reader to buy a certain product or think about an important topic.

In a persuasive paragraph, you must give your **opinion**. Your opinion is what you think, feel, and believe. You must give facts to show that your opinion is one that others should agree with.

Here are some hints that will make your persuasive paragraph stronger.

- Choose a topic that you feel strongly about.
- Choose an audience.
- State your opinion in the topic sentence.
- In the detail sentences, give three reasons or facts why a reader should agree with you.
- State your opinion again or ask the reader to do something in the concluding sentence.

Here is an example of a persuasive paragraph.

I think the library needs to buy more computers. Right now, there are four computers to use. Many people use the computers to check e-mail, type reports, and research information. With only four computers available, people always have to wait. If the library gets more computers, more people can use them.

Follow the directions below.

1. Think about problems that you would like to fix. Write a list of three of them.

   _____

   _____

   _____

2. Which problem do you feel the strongest about? Circle it.

78

Persuasive Paragraph, continued

Use the Prewriting Survey on pages 108–109 to plan your persuasive paragraph. Complete the organizer you chose on the survey to help you find more details. Then answer the questions below.

1. What is your opinion of the problem?

   _____

2. What are some words that tell how you feel about the problem?

   _____

3. Why is there a problem?

   _____

4. Why is the problem bad? List three reasons or details.

   Reason 1 _____

   Reason 2 _____

   Reason 3 _____

5. Which reason is the most important? Circle it.

6. Who is your audience? _____

7. What words could you use to get the reader to think the way that you do?

   _____

8. What will you ask the reader to do? _____

   _____

WRITE AWAY

You have thought about a problem that you feel strongly about. You have listed ideas in the prewriting step. Now it's time to start your draft. Use another sheet of paper. Review the hints on page 78. Then follow the rest of the steps in the writing process to write your persuasive paragraph.

Information Paragraph

In many science or social studies activities, you often have to write a paragraph telling about one topic. This kind of paragraph is an **information paragraph**. It includes two or three details about the topic. The details should be facts, or true pieces of information, and not opinions about the topic. For example, if you write about the sun, you might include the fact that it is a star. You would not include an opinion that you like the sun.

To write a good information paragraph

- Choose one topic.
- Write a topic sentence that states the main idea.
- Write at least two detail sentences that include facts about the topic.
- Write a concluding sentence.
- Be sure your facts are correct. Do not include your opinions.
- Think of a title for your information paragraph.
- Add a picture to show information about what you are writing.

Here is an example of an information paragraph.

Turtles Stay Safe

A turtle is an animal that has a hard shell. The shell protects the soft inside of the turtle. When the turtle feels scared, it pulls its head, legs, and tail inside the shell. No other animal can get inside. The turtle will come outside again when it is safe.

What topic do you know about? Use the Prewriting Survey on pages 108–109 to plan an information paragraph on your topic. Compete the organizer you chose on the survey to help plan the paragraph.

Information Paragraph, continued

An information paragraph needs linking words and phrases to connect ideas. Linking words and phrases are transition words and time-order words. Here are some examples you can use to write an information paragraph.

also	another	more	in addition
but	since	and	for example

Here is another example of an information paragraph. Pay attention to the linking words and phrases.

Our Lady Liberty

The Statue of Liberty is a symbol of United States freedom. She was a birthday gift from France. France gave "Lady Liberty" to the United States on July 4, 1884. A French sculptor worked very hard to carve the Statue of Liberty. <u>Also</u>, he worked very long hours. <u>For example</u>, <u>since</u> she was such a large statue, it took him 21 years to complete the project! Millions of people have visited the Statue of Liberty.

Use the hints above to review the parts of a good information paragraph. Then write a draft of your information paragraph on another sheet of paper. Use the information in the organizer you chose on the Prewriting Survey.

Information Paragraph, continued

It's time to focus on revising your information paragraph to make it clearer or more interesting. Read the tips below.

Ways to Revise

- Add words, phrases, or sentences.
- Delete information you don't need.
- Choose words that make your writing clear.
- Combine short, choppy sentences.
- Add linking words for smooth transitions.

Now read the revised paragraph about turtles.

Turtles Stay Safe

What must an animal like a turtle do to stay safe? First of all, a turtle has a hard shell. The tough shell protects the soft inside of the turtle so it can stay safe. When the turtle feels scared, it has another way to protect itself. The turtle pulls its head, legs, and tail inside the shell. No other animal can get inside. After a while, the turtle will come outside again when it is safe.

Use the hints above to review the parts of a good information paragraph. Then follow the steps in the writing process to revise and proofread the draft you wrote on page 81.

Information Paragraph, continued

You have followed the first four steps in the writing process. Now it's time to publish your information paragraph. Here are some questions to help you present your work.

1. Read the paragraph. Which words are the most important? Write three.

   _____

2. How can you use these words to make a title? Write several ideas.

   _____

3. Who is your audience?

   _____

4. What are some ways to show your work to this reader? (notebook paper, printer paper, computer printing, booklet, etc.)

   _____

5. Which way will make the reader say, "WOW!" Why?

   _____

6. What kind of picture can you include on the page? A picture might be a drawing, map, diagram, or time line. Remember that a picture makes the main idea or a detail clearer.

   _____

7. Where is the best place to put the picture on the page? Why?

   _____

WRITE AWAY

On another sheet of paper, publish your information paragraph. You can also use the tips on pages 116–117 to publish your work on a computer. Use the answers above to help you show your work in the best way. You may want to read it aloud one more time before you share it!

Compare and Contrast Paragraph

Which do you prefer—hot dogs or hamburgers? Both kinds of meat are tasty on a bun. You can squirt ketchup and mustard on them, too. But a hamburger is round, and a hot dog is long and skinny. They also taste different. So which do you like better?

The paragraph above compares and contrasts hamburgers and hot dogs. When you show how two things are alike, you compare them. When you show how they are different, you contrast them. Looking at how people, places, and things are alike and different helps you understand more about them.

Here are some hints that will make the topics in a compare and contrast paragraph easier to understand.

- Write a topic sentence that identifies the two people, places, or things.
- Tell how the two are alike. Give examples.
- Use words to give a clue that you are comparing them, such as *both, same, also,* and *alike*.
- Tell how the two are different. Give examples.
- Use words to give a clue that you are contrasting them, such as *different, but,* and *however*.
- Write about the topics in the same order as they are listed in the topic sentence.

Here is an example of a compare and contrast paragraph.

Kelly and Jim are friends. They both like to paint. They also like to read. However, Kelly is different from Jim. Kelly likes to play soccer. Jim does not. Jim would rather play basketball.

Think about a friend. How are you the same as and different from this friend? Use the Prewriting Survey on pages 108–109 to plan a compare and contrast paragraph about both of you. Complete the organizer you chose on the survey to help plan the paragraph. Then look at the hints above to review the parts of a good compare and contrast paragraph. Next, follow the steps in the writing process to write a draft and revise it. Use another sheet of paper.

Compare and Contrast Paragraph, continued

You have followed three steps in the writing process. Now it is time to proofread your work. The questions below will help you complete this step.

1. Read your paragraph. What proper nouns are in it? Do they all begin with a

   capital letter? _____

2. How many sentences are in your paragraph? Do they all begin with a capital letter?

   _____

3. How many questions did you write? Do they end with a question mark?

   _____

4. Do all other sentences have the correct end mark? How do you know?

   _____

5. Did you write a list of three or more things? If so, did you use a comma to separate

   those items in the list? _____

6. Remember that homophones are words that sound the same but have different spellings and meanings. *To, too,* and *two* are homophones. Which homophones did you use in your writing?

   _____

7. Which words might be spelled incorrectly? Look them up in a dictionary.

   _____

WRITE AWAY

Use the questions above to help you proofread your paragraph. Then publish it on another sheet of paper. You can also use the tips on pages 116–117 to publish your work on a computer. Share the paragraph with the friend that you wrote about.

Poem

You've spent a lot of time working on writing paragraphs. Now it is time to change gears and try a new and fun form—writing a **poem**! In a poem the writer paints a picture with words. Poems can be written in a variety of ways. They can tell about how a writer feels, describe how things are alike and different, or describe something in an unusual way. Most poems have rhyming words, but they do not have to.

Here are some hints that will make writing a poem fun.

- Choose a topic that you feel strongly about.
- Choose colorful words that paint a picture of the topic.
- Use rhyming words and rhythm if you want.
- Tell how things are alike.
- Tell how things are different.
- Write a title that grabs the reader's attention.

Here are two examples of poems that have the same topic. One rhymes, and one does not.

Cat and Mouse

The mouse poked out her tiny head.
"Look and listen," her mother said.
She heard a bell, and that was that.
The clever mouse escaped the cat.

Cat and Mouse

Like a guard watching for danger,
The mouse peeked around for the cat.
Like an alarm ringing out a warning,
The cat's bell signaled the mouse.
As quick as an eye can blink,
The mouse disappeared.

Follow the directions below.

1. What is your favorite season? Why?

_____

_____

2. On another sheet of paper, draw a picture that goes with the sentence you wrote above.

Poem, continued

Use the Prewriting Survey on pages 108–109 to plan your poem. Complete the organizer you chose on the survey to help you think about your poem. Then answer the questions below. They will help you write a poem.

1. What are some things that you see in your favorite season? Think about animals and what is happening in nature. Write at least four words.

   _____

2. Choose one word above. Compare it to something else that is very different. Tell how they are alike using word pictures.

   _____

3. What do you feel during this time of year? Write four adjectives.

   _____

4. Choose one of the words above. Brainstorm a list of rhyming words for this word.

   Try to name at least ten words. _____

   _____

5. Choose another word from question 1 or 3. What are some words that begin with the same sound that tell more about the season?

   _____

6. Think of some sounds you might hear during this time of year. What words tell about these sounds? For example, the wind might *swoosh*, or a bee might *buzz*.

   _____

WRITE AWAY

You have been prewriting ideas for a poem. You have lots of things to write about now! Review the hints on page 86. They will help you paint a word picture. Then follow the rest of the steps in the writing process. Try to write a poem that is at least six lines long. It can rhyme, but it doesn't have to. It's your choice! Use another sheet of paper.

Friendly Letter

A **friendly letter** is a letter that is sent to someone the writer knows. The message often includes news that the reader would find interesting.

There are five parts of a friendly letter: a heading, greeting, body, closing, and signature. The example below shows these parts.

heading ⌐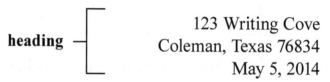

                                    123 Writing Cove
                                    Coleman, Texas 76834
                                    May 5, 2014

greeting ⌐ Dear Aunt Sally,

body ⌐   Mother finally let me get a puppy! We went to the animal
                shelter today. I looked at all the puppies, and I picked out one
                that had stripes. I knew it was the one for me because it licked
                my face when I picked it up. I will call my new puppy Tiger.
                You will see Tiger when you come visit next month.

closing ⌐   Your nephew,

signature ⌐   Gino

Here are some hints to help you write a great friendly letter.
- Choose your audience, or the person to whom you will write.
- Write your address and the date in the heading.
- End the greeting with a comma.
- In the body, write information that the reader will find interesting.
- The first word in the closing begins with a capital letter. Other words begin with a lowercase letter. End the closing with a comma.
- Sign your name beneath the closing.

Choose a person to whom you could write a friendly letter. Use the Prewriting Survey on pages 108–109 to plan the message. Complete the organizer you chose on the survey to help plan it. Then look at the hints. Next follow the steps in the writing process. Write a draft and revise it. Use another sheet of paper.

Friendly Letter, continued

You have followed the first three steps in the writing process. Now it is time to proofread your letter. Answer the questions below to check your letter.

1. What city and state did you write in the heading? Do they begin with a capital letter? Did you write a comma between the names?

   _____

2. What mark did you write between the names of the city and state? What mark did you write between the date and the year?

   _____

3. What greeting did you write? Does each word begin with a capital letter?

   _____

4. What mark did you write at the end of the greeting?

   _____

5. How many sentences did you write? Do they all begin with capital letters? Do they all have an end mark?

   _____

6. How many words did you write in the closing? Does only the first word begin with a capital letter?

   _____

7. What mark did you write at the end of the closing?

   _____

8. Which words might be spelled incorrectly? Look them up in the dictionary.

   _____

   _____

WRITE AWAY

Use the questions above to help you proofread your letter. Publish it on another sheet of paper. You can also use the tips on pages 116–117 to publish your work on a computer. Then send the letter to the person you wrote.

Book Report

A **book report** shares information about a book you have read. It tells the most important information, such as the author, the main characters, the setting, and the main idea, without giving away the ending. The report also shares your opinion of the book and tells if other people might like to read it.

Here are some hints that will help you write a book report.
- Include the title of the book in the topic sentence. Underline it.
- Give the author's name, the setting, and the main characters.
- Summarize the book without giving too many details.
- Give your opinion of the book.
- Provide reasons to support your opinion.
- Use linking words and phrases (*because, therefore, since, for example*).
- Tell who might like to read the book.
- Write a title for the book report.
- Write a concluding sentence the sums up the information.

Here is an example of a book report.

A Whale of a Story

The book Humphrey the Lost Whale by Wendy Tokuda and Richard Hall is the best book ever! It tells the amazing but true story of a young whale that took a wrong turn. In the book, people were at first surprised and pleased to see a whale in San Francisco Bay. Then Humphrey headed up the Sacramento River. People soon realized he was lost and wanted to help. For example, hundreds of people worked together to get Humphrey back to the ocean. I think this story will make you cheer. Read this fascinating book and share it with a friend.

WRITE AWAY

1. What book would you like to tell a friend about? Why?

_____

_____

2. Why would your friend like to know about this book?

_____

90

Book Report, continued

Use the Prewriting Survey on pages 108–109 to plan your book report. Complete the organizer you chose on the survey to help you plan your report. Then answer the questions below.

1. What is the title of the book? _____

2. Who wrote the book? _____

3. Who is the main character in the book? _____

   _____

4. Where does the book take place? _____

5. What is the main idea of the book? _____

   _____

6. What are three important events in the book? _____

   _____

   _____

7. What is your opinion of the book? _____

   _____

8. What reasons support your opinion? _____

   _____

9. What book report title would catch the interest of your audience?

   _____

WRITE AWAY

You have been prewriting ideas for a book report. Review the hints on page 90 and then begin your draft. Follow the rest of the steps in the writing process. Publish your book report on another sheet of paper. You can also use the tips on pages 116–117 to publish your work on a computer. Then share your report with friends. They might want to read the book, too.

Name _____ Date _____

Opinion Paragraph

An **opinion paragraph** tells what a writer thinks or feels about a topic. An opinion paragraph includes reasons to support the writer's opinion. Reasons explain why the writer has a certain opinion. Facts, details, and examples support the reasons for the writer's opinion. You can also include a picture or other drawing to help the reader understand your opinion.

Here are some hints that will make your opinion paragraph even better.
- Choose one topic.
- Write a sentence that tells your opinion about the topic.
- Write one or two reasons to support your opinion. Tell why you feel the way you do about the topic.
- Write two or more detail sentences to support and explain each reason.
- Write a concluding sentence. Repeat the opinion in a new way.
- Use linking words and phrases (*because, therefore, since, for example*).

Here is an example of an opinion paragraph.

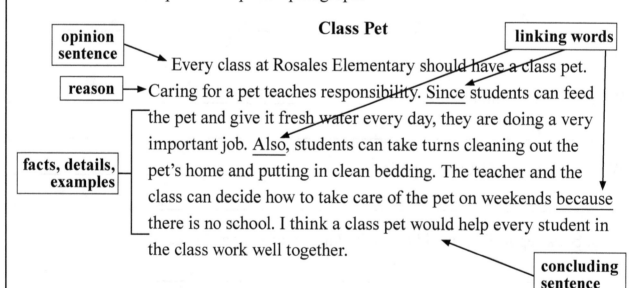

Class Pet

| opinion sentence | Every class at Rosales Elementary should have a class pet. |

linking words

| reason | Caring for a pet teaches responsibility. Since students can feed the pet and give it fresh water every day, they are doing a very important job. Also, students can take turns cleaning out the pet's home and putting in clean bedding. The teacher and the class can decide how to take care of the pet on weekends because there is no school. I think a class pet would help every student in the class work well together. |

facts, details, examples

concluding sentence

Follow the directions below.

1. What topics do you feel strongly about? List three topics.

_____

_____

2. Which topic above can you support with two reasons? Circle it.

Opinion Paragraph, continued

> The topic sentence introduces the writer's opinion. The final sentence restates and reminds readers of the opinion. The same opinion is stated in both, using different words. A good concluding statement makes a final comment and wraps up the ideas.
>
> **Topic:** Class activity
>
> **Opinion sentence:** Learning about how to take care of a dog as a pet was interesting.
>
> **Concluding sentence:** It was a lot of fun to learn about the different things a dog owner needs to do for his or her pet.

Work with another student to write a topic sentence and a concluding sentence about the topics below.

1. Topic: movie

   Opinion sentence: _____

   Concluding sentence: _____

2. Topic: food

   Opinion sentence: _____

   Concluding sentence: _____

3. Topic: field trips

   Opinion sentence: _____

   Concluding sentence: _____

WRITE AWAY

On another sheet of paper, write an opinion sentence and a concluding sentence for the topic you circled on page 92.

Opinion Paragraph, continued

When you choose a topic, decide what you believe about that topic. For example, you might write about favorite days or holidays. Perhaps you think that the first day of school is your favorite day. Your opinion will be the first sentence. Then you need to decide which two or three reasons you can use to support your first sentence.

Topic: favorite days

Opinion statement: The first day of school is my favorite day of the year.

Reason 1: I'm always excited and nervous to meet my teacher and see my classroom.

Reason 2: I get to see old friends and make new ones.

Read each of the topics below. Write one opinion sentence for each topic. Write two reasons to support the opinion.

1. heroes

    Opinion sentence: _____

    Reason 1: _____

    Reason 2: _____

2. school activities

    Opinion sentence: _____

    Reason 1: _____

    Reason 2: _____

WRITE AWAY

Think about the opinion sentence you wrote for your topic. On another sheet of paper, write two reasons that support your opinion sentence.

Opinion Paragraph, continued

You've come up with reasons for your opinion. Now think of facts and details that support each reason. Notice how the writer of this opinion paragraph has facts and details that support the reasons. The writer tells the most important reason first. The last sentence sums up the writer's opinion.

Keeping Rover Safe

I think dogs should be kept on leashes at all times when they are outside, especially in public places. One reason is that a leash helps an owner keep his or her dog close. The dog is not able to run over to a dog that it does not know. The other dog may not like being around strange dogs. A dog on a leash cannot run into a busy street with lots of traffic.

Also, a leash helps keep a dog from hurting others. For example, it is less likely to bite a person or knock over a small child. Leashes are an important way to keep dogs safe.

Write your reasons for your topic from page 94. Then write a fact or detail that supports each reason.

Reason 1: _____

_____

Fact or detail that supports the reason: _____

Reason 2: _____

_____

Fact or detail that supports the reason: _____

WRITE AWAY

You have decided on a topic and have written an opinion sentence and a concluding sentence. You have written reasons and facts and details. Now it is time to start your draft on another sheet of paper. Review the hints on page 92. Then follow the rest of the steps in the writing process to write your opinion paragraph. You can handwrite your final copy or use the tips on pages 116–117 to publish your work on a computer.

Short Report

You have already written an information paragraph. You can use this knowledge to help you write a **short report**. A short report is a form of writing made up of several information paragraphs. Each paragraph has a main idea that tells more about a topic.

When you write a short report, you will have to find facts about the topic. You can find the facts using different **resources**, such as books, encyclopedias, magazines, or articles on the Internet. Then you will have to take notes on the facts. You will learn how to take notes on the next page.

Here are some hints to help you write a short report.

- Choose a topic that has at least three main ideas.
- Find three details about each main idea.
- Include only facts about the topic.
- Take notes about the facts.
- In the first paragraph of the report, identify the topic.
- Write one paragraph for each main idea.
- Write one last paragraph that summarizes all the information.
- Write a title for your report.

Follow the directions.

1. What topic would you like to know more about? List three ideas.

   _____

   _____

   _____

2. Which topic above do you think has three main ideas? Circle it.

WRITE AWAY

You will need to see if your topic has enough information. With the help of a family member or friend, go to the library or look on the Internet. Find the three main ideas that you will use. Write them on another sheet of paper. If you find that the topic is too big or too small, you can focus on a different part of the topic, or you can choose one of the other topics you listed above.

Name _____ Date _____

Short Report, continued

It is important to find facts that tell about your topic. You will need to look in one or more resources to find these details. You can **take notes** to help you remember the information. Here are some hints to help you take notes.

- Write questions about that topic. Then find the answers in a resource.
- Write the title of the resource, the author, and the pages where you found the fact. Underline the title of the resource.
- Write only the fact that answers the question.
- Write the information in your own words.

Writers often write their notes on **note cards**. They write one question on each card. By doing so, they can organize the cards to help them plan their report. Here is a sample note card.

> Where do monarch butterflies migrate?
>
> On Butterfly Wings by Dr. Agnes Insect
>
> Page 82
>
> Butterflies migrate to Mexico or California in the winter. They fly all over the United States and into Canada in the summer.

Think about the main ideas you chose for your topic. What information do you need in your report? Write two questions.

_____

_____

WRITE AWAY

With the help of a family member, go to the library or look on the Internet. Take notes about your topic. You can use the Note Cards on page 124, or you can use your own paper or cards. Remember that you must find three details about each main idea.

Short Report, continued

Now you need to organize your report. Sort your note cards into groups. Put all the details that tell about the same main idea together. Each group will form one paragraph of the report.

Read the information on each group of cards. Thank about the best order to tell the facts in the paragraph. Put the cards in that order. Use the **outline** below to show the order of the paragraphs and the information.

Complete the outline.

Topic of the Report: _____

Main Idea of Paragraph 1: _____

Detail: _____

Detail: _____

Detail: _____

Main Idea of Paragraph 2: _____

Detail: _____

Detail: _____

Detail: _____

Main Idea of Paragraph 3: _____

Detail: _____

Detail: _____

Detail: _____

WRITE AWAY

You have finished prewriting your short report! Review the hints on page 96. Then follow the rest of the steps of the writing process to write your report. Publish your final copy on another sheet of paper. You can also use the tips on pages 116–117 to publish your work on a computer.

Name _____ Date _____

Biography

You have probably written about a famous person. Maybe you wrote about Abraham Lincoln or George Washington Carver. Did you know that you were writing a **biography**?

A biography is a special kind of short report. It is a true story of someone's life that is written by another person. It tells the most important events that happened to this person. Many biographies are about famous people, but they do not have to be. You can write a biography that tells about the life of someone that is special to you.

Here are some hints that will help you write a good biography.

- Find facts about the person. Write these facts in your own words.
- Include dates to help the reader understand the time.
- Summarize the key life events.
- Tell why this person is special.

Here are some example paragraphs from a biography.

George Washington Carver—The Peanut Man

Do you drink cherry punch? Have you ever painted a house? If so, you have one man to thank—George Washington Carver. He found that peanuts could be used to make these goods.

Carver was born in 1864. He was a slave. Carver was very curious and taught himself how to read and write. He found out that there was a school that African American children could go to. It was eight miles away. That did not stop Carver. He walked to and from school every day.

Follow the directions below.

1. Who are some people that you would like to know more about? Name two.

_____

_____

2. Who do you think would be the most fun to write about? Circle that name.

Biography, continued

Before writing a biography, you will have to find facts about the person. Follow the prewriting steps for a short report found on pages 96–98. The questions below will also help you gather the important details.

1. When and where was this person born?

   _____

2. What did this person do that makes him or her special?

   _____

   _____

3. What are some important events in this person's life? Fill in the time line. Be sure to include the year.

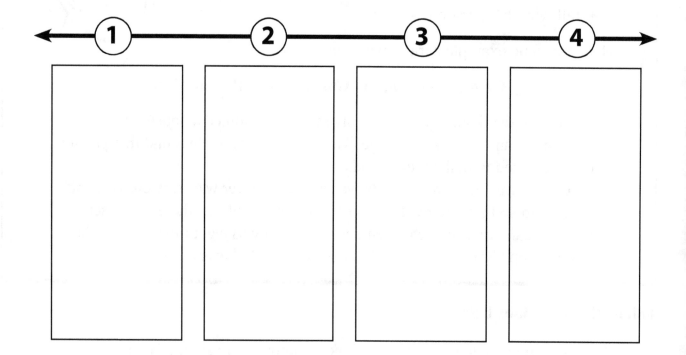

WRITE AWAY

Follow the steps in the writing process to write a biography. Then write your final copy on another sheet of paper. You can also use the tips on pages 116–117 to publish your final copy on a computer.

Short Story

Finally! Here is the lesson that you have been waiting for—the **short story**. A short story is a story that tells about made-up characters. Short stories are fun to read. They allow you to visit other lands and meet different characters. Short stories can be fun to write, too. But before you begin to write, you will need to think about the different parts that make up each story.

- The **characters** are the people or animals in the story. They are make-believe.
- The **setting** is where and when the story takes place.
- The **plot** is the series of actions in the story. The plot begins because there is a **problem** that the characters must solve.
- The story has a clear **sequence of events**. This means that the story events are told in order. For example, the story has a clear beginning, middle, and end. The characters, setting, and problem are introduced at the beginning of the story. The characters try to solve the problem in the middle. The characters solve the problem at the end.

You'll take a closer look at each of these parts in the next four pages. Along the way, you will plan your story. The prewriting for a short story is a little different from the other forms of writing. There are many details to think about. But by the time you are done, you will have the start of an exciting story!

Think about the story "The Three Bears." Answer the questions.

1. Who are the main characters? _____

_____

2. What is the setting? _____

3. What is the problem? _____

_____

4. What is one event that happens in the middle of the story?

_____

5. How is the problem solved? _____

_____

Short Story, continued

To write a story, you need to begin with an idea. So how can you get an idea for a great story? You can get one anywhere. You might see something funny while you are shopping in the mall. You might have a dream. Something might happen to you that would make a great story if you changed a few of the details.

For this story, you will get ideas from a **setting** you choose. Remember that the setting is where and when a short story takes place. A farm, outer space, or an old house can be the setting. The story can take place long ago, yesterday, on a sunny day, in the winter, or one hundred years in the future.

A setting can also affect the feeling of the story. If the story takes place at a circus, it will probably be a funny story. If the story takes place in an old house on a rainy night, it might be a scary story.

Answer the questions below to help you choose a story setting.

1. Where might your story take place? Circle one.

    zoo   farm   garden   palace

    park   school   playground   lake

    space   pet store   other _____

2. What year is it? Circle one.

    long ago   now   in the future   other _____

3. What season is it? What is the weather like?_____

4. What feeling do you want the story to have? _____

5. How can you use your senses to know more about the setting?

    See _____   Touch _____

    Taste _____   Smell _____

    Hear _____

Short Story, continued

Now that you have thought about a setting, the next step is to think about a **problem**. The problem gets the story action going. Short stories use both real and make-believe details. In most stories, the problem is something that could happen. Readers are more likely to read a story that they can believe.

Before you choose a problem, you should also think about the feeling you want in your story. Think about a circus story. If the feeling is supposed to be happy, would you want someone to get hurt? Probably not! You would want to have a silly problem. Perhaps a circus dog takes a clown's shoes. The clown has to get them back before the show begins!

Think about the feeling and setting that you want your story to have. Then answer the questions below to help you choose a problem.

1. What are two problems that could happen to help readers feel this way?

   _____

   _____

2. What could characters do to solve the first problem?

   _____

3. What could characters do to solve the second problem?

   _____

4. Which problem do you think readers would find the most interesting? Why?

   _____

   _____

5. Tell what you know about your story so far.

   Setting—where _____

   Setting—when _____

   Problem _____

103

Short Story, continued

Choosing **characters** is the next step in planning your story. The characters are the people and animals in the story. In a short story, they are all made up. But some characters seem real. They are human. They talk and act like people. On the other hand, some characters are animals. They might act like animals or people.

When you choose characters, you need to think about what they will be like. Are they happy and helpful? Are they bossy? Do they talk too much? How a character acts can affect how the problem gets solved. Think once again about the circus setting where the dog takes the clown's shoes. A bossy clown might make the dog run to many different places in the circus tent. A helpful clown could offer to trade many interesting things for the shoes.

Knowing what characters are like will also affect how they think, act, and talk. Dialogue is what the characters say. **Dialogue** moves the plot along. **Description** includes details that tell what a character thinks or feels. Dialogue and description give more information about what the characters are like. A bossy clown would give commands. A helpful clown would speak kindly.

Answer the questions below to help you choose a main character.

1. Is the main character a human or an animal? If you choose an animal, does it act like

   an animal or a human? _____

2. What is the main character like? Circle as many adjectives as you want.

   friendly   mean   grumpy   happy   angry   shy   scared

   quiet   smart   talkative   silly   old   young   bossy

3. What does this character look like? Use lively adjectives.

   _____

4. What could the character say in dialogue that shows what he or she is like?

   _____

5. What other characters might be in the story? What will they do?

   _____

104

Short Story, continued

It is time to think about the **plot** of your short story. The plot is what happens in the story. The plot starts because of a problem. The problem unfolds through a sequence of events. The **sequence of events** includes the beginning, middle, and end of the story.

Think back to what you learned about transition words and time-order words. Your short story will flow smoothly if you use these words. For example, *once upon a time, the next day, then,* and *finally* help the reader follow the events in the story.

Answer the questions below to help you plan your story plot.

Beginning

1. Where does the story take place? _____

2. Who is the main character? _____

Middle

3. What is the problem? _____

    _____

4. What happens first in the story? _____

    _____

5. What happens next in the story? _____

    _____

End

6. How is the problem solved? _____

    _____

7. Does the end wrap up the story? _____

WRITE AWAY

You have been prewriting your story. Now it's time to write the draft on another sheet of paper. Don't worry about mistakes. Just write! Keep your prewriting ideas next to you and look at them often. They will help you include all the important parts.

Short Story, continued

Revising your draft is the next step in writing your short story.
As you revise, you need to look at it through the eyes of your audience.
The ideas below can help you look at the work with a new point of view.

Look at your draft. Use the questions below to revise your short story.

1. Does the opening sentence catch the reader's attention? Explain.

   _____

2. What does your character do that makes him or her seem real?

   _____

3. What words do you use to describe the main character? Is the description clear?

   _____

4. Do the events in the plot happen in an order that makes sense? If not, what can you
   add or change to help a reader understand the plot better?

   _____

5. Do you have short, medium, and long sentences to make the story flow smoothly?

   _____

6. Is the problem solved in a way that makes sense to a reader? Explain.

   _____

7. What do you want your reader to remember the most about this story?

   _____

WRITE AWAY

The questions above will help you revise your short story. Use the answers as a guide to
rewrite the story. Then follow the rest of the steps in the writing process. Write your final
copy on another sheet of paper. You can also use the tips on pages 116–117 to publish your
final copy on a computer. Don't forget to add a picture or two when you publish
your work!

Name ———————————————————— Date ———————————

Journal Entry

Date ————————————————————

Dear Journal,

——————————————————————————————————

——————————————————————————————————

——————————————————————————————————

——————————————————————————————————

——————————————————————————————————

——————————————————————————————————

——————————————————————————————————

——————————————————————————————————

——————————————————————————————————

Prewriting Survey

My Purpose

1. What am I writing about?

   _____

2. What do I want to say?

   _____

   _____

3. What is my purpose for writing? Explain.

   _____

   _____

My Audience

4. Who will be reading my writing? What do I know about the people who will read what I write?

   _____

   _____

5. What does my audience already know about my topic? What new information will I tell my audience?

   _____

   _____

6. How will I share my writing with my audience?

   _____

   _____

Prewriting Survey, continued

Writing Purpose and Details

7. Why am I writing? Choose one purpose below and write the details you want to share.

To inform (to give facts about a topic)	Who What Where	When Why How
To express (to share a feeling or idea)	What I see What I hear What I touch What I smell What I taste	
To entertain (to make the reader experience an emotion)	Feelings Strong words Stories Memories	
To persuade (to make the reader think or act a certain way)	My opinion A fact that supports my opinion A fact that supports my opinion A fact that supports my opinion	

Writing Pattern

8. Which writing pattern will I use to achieve my purpose?

Main idea and details   Sequence of events   Compare and contrast

Problem and solution   Cause and effect   Summary

Planning

9. Which graphic organizer can help me plan the details of my writing? Circle all that you could use.

Main idea and details web   Sequence chart   Cause and effect chart

Problem and solution chart   Venn diagram   Summary chart

109

Writing Traits Checklist

Title _____

Trait	Strong	Average	Needs Improvement
Ideas			
The main idea of my writing is interesting.			
The main idea is clear.			
I use details that tell about the main idea.			
Organization			
The form of writing makes the information clear.			
There is a beginning, a middle, and an end.			
The details are in the right order.			
I use words to connect my ideas.			
My first sentence catches the reader's interest.			
My last sentence states the main idea in a different way.			
Voice			
I show what I think or feel about the topic.			
I show my feelings in my writing.			
I use words that readers will understand.			
Word Choice			
I use the five senses to describe things.			
I use strong action words to tell what is happening.			
I use a variety of words in my writing.			
I use new words in my writing.			

Writing Traits Checklist, continued

Trait	Strong	Average	Needs Improvement
Sentence Fluency			
I have sentences that are short, medium, and long.			
I write sentences that have different patterns.			
Conventions			
All sentences begin with a capital letter.			
All my sentences have an end mark.			
I use an apostrophe to show when something belongs to someone.			
I use a comma correctly with dates and addresses.			
I use a comma to separate items in a list.			
Proper nouns begin with capital letters.			
I use quotation marks when someone says something.			
All words are spelled correctly.			
I indent paragraphs.			
I put space between my words.			
I write from left to right.			
Presentation			
My writing has a title.			
I use pictures or diagrams to help show ideas in my writing.			
The final copy is clean and neat.			

Writing Interest Survey

1. How often do you like to read? Check one.

    ☐ often   ☐ not often

    ☐ sometimes   ☐ never

2. What is your favorite book? Why is it your favorite book?

    _____

    _____

3. What genres do you like to read? Check as many as you want.

    ☐ newspapers   ☐ magazines   ☐ biography   ☐ poetry

    ☐ science fiction ☐ adventure   ☐ fantasy   ☐ mystery

    ☐ historical fiction ☐ humor   ☐ realistic fiction

    ☐ nonfiction (What kinds?) _____

    ☐ other _____

4. What would you like to do better as a reader?

    ☐ understand what I read   ☐ read faster

    ☐ read harder books   ☐ other _____

5. When you write, how do you like to work?

    ☐ in a large group   ☐ in pairs

    ☐ in a small group   ☐ alone

112

Writing Interest Survey, continued

6. How often do you like to write? Check one.

☐ less than once a week

☐ 1 to 2 times per week

☐ 3 to 4 times per week

☐ every day (7 times a week)

7. What kinds of writing do you like to do? Check as many as you want.

☐ true stories   ☐ letters   ☐ poems   ☐ journal or diary

☐ reports   ☐ articles   ☐ songs   ☐ research papers

☐ fiction stories   ☐ realistic fiction   ☐ mysteries   ☐ riddles

☐ other _____

8. What do you like most about writing?

_____

_____

_____

_____

9. What do you like least about writing?

_____

_____

_____

_____

Proofreading Checklist

It is important to proofread your work before you publish it. When you proofread, you take another look at your writing for mistakes. You should read your work once for capital letters. You should read it a second time for end marks and commas. You should read it a third time for spelling. Then trade papers with a partner for a final proofreading. This list will help you proofread.

Capitalization

☐ Do all sentences begin with a capital letter?

☐ Are titles and people's names capitalized?

☐ Are names of particular places capitalized?

☐ Are the months and days of the week capitalized?

Punctuation

☐ Does each sentence have an end mark (period, question mark, exclamation mark)?

☐ Is there a period at the end of each abbreviation?

☐ Does a comma separate items in a list?

☐ Is a comma correctly used with dates and addresses?

☐ Does a comma correctly separate a quotation from the rest of the sentence?

☐ Are quotation marks correctly used around the words that people say?

☐ Does an apostrophe correctly show when something belongs to someone?

Spelling

☐ Are all the words spelled correctly?

☐ Did I use a dictionary to check words that may not be spelled correctly?

☐ Did I use a dictionary to check troublesome words?

Proofreading Marks

Use these special marks to show the mistakes in your writing.

≡	Use a capital letter.
⊙	Add a period.
∧	Add something.
⋏	Add a comma.
ⱽⱽ	Add quotation marks.
ℐ	Cut something.
⋏	Replace something.
⁀	Transpose.
◯	Spell correctly.
¶	Indent paragraph.
/	Make a lowercase letter.

Name _____   Date _____

Publishing Your Writing

Publishing is the last step in the writing process. There are many ways you can use technology to write. You can use e-mail to send your writing to anyone who has an e-mail address. An e-mail is like a letter. Be sure you have the e-mail address of the person you want to send it to.

Always ask an adult before you use a computer. Ask an adult or a friend if you need help.

The boxes below tell what information to include in an e-mail.

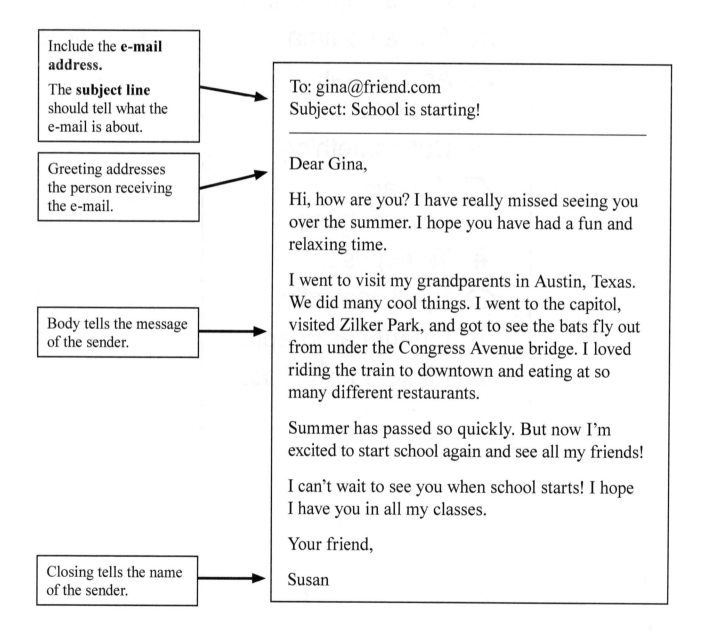

Include the **e-mail address.**

The **subject line** should tell what the e-mail is about.

Greeting addresses the person receiving the e-mail.

Body tells the message of the sender.

Closing tells the name of the sender.

To: gina@friend.com
Subject: School is starting!

Dear Gina,

Hi, how are you? I have really missed seeing you over the summer. I hope you have had a fun and relaxing time.

I went to visit my grandparents in Austin, Texas. We did many cool things. I went to the capitol, visited Zilker Park, and got to see the bats fly out from under the Congress Avenue bridge. I loved riding the train to downtown and eating at so many different restaurants.

Summer has passed so quickly. But now I'm excited to start school again and see all my friends!

I can't wait to see you when school starts! I hope I have you in all my classes.

Your friend,

Susan

116

Publishing Your Writing, continued

Blog Post

The word **blog** is short for "weblog." A blog is a journal that you keep on the Internet so that other people can read and comment. You can use a blog to share news about yourself with others. Blogs can also be essays or include opinions. You can publish your writing for class on your class blog. Ask your teacher to show you how to publish to your class blog. Notice the important parts of a blog.

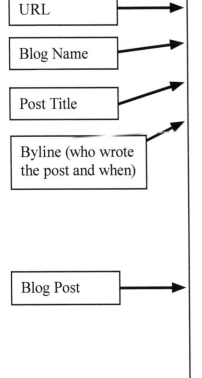

URL → **http:/www.—.com/blog**

Blog Name → **Mr. Chung's 3rd Grade Class Blog**

Post Title → **Small things can make a big difference for children and families**

Byline (who wrote the post and when) → **by Rosa on February 19, 2013 at 2:45pm**

Blog Post →

Our school has begun a contest to collect loose change for the Ronald McDonald House in our city. The class at each grade level that collects the most change will get to visit and tour the House.

The Ronald McDonald House gives families a place to stay near their children who are in the hospital. Families are able to sleep, eat, and relax while their children receive treatment in a nearby hospital. The House is a home away from home for families who live 25 or more miles outside of our city.

Guest families make a $10 donation per night. However, if a donation cannot be made, families can still stay at the House.

My school is excited to see how many nights our loose change will provide for guest families. We challenge other schools in our city to collect change for this wonderful organization. Or go to their Web site, rmhc–yourcity.org, for more information on other ways to volunteer.

Comments

Name of Reader Leaving Comment → Mrs. Luna

Thank you for telling us about this problem, Rosa. I wonder if there is a way the class can help. Let's look into this together!

Main Idea and Details Web

Write the main idea in the oval. Write four strong details in the circles. Think about specific and lively words that you could use in your writing to tell about the details. Add these words in the rectangles.

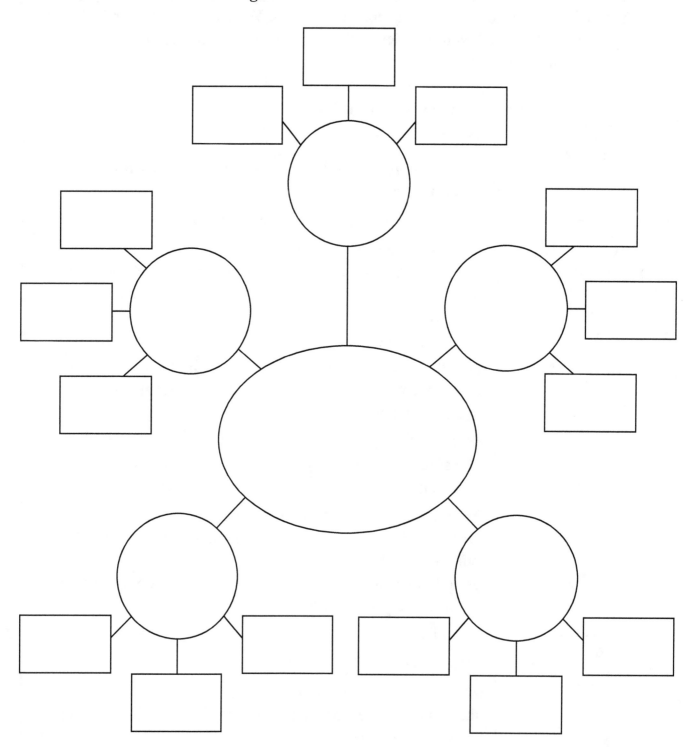

Sequence Chart

Write the steps or events in the order they happen. Write time-order words on the lines to help you explain the order.

First, _____

_____ ,

_____ ,

_____ ,

Finally, _____

119

Venn Diagram

Write the names of the things you are comparing on the lines above the circles. In the overlapping space, tell how the things are the same. In the rest of the circles, tell how each thing is different.

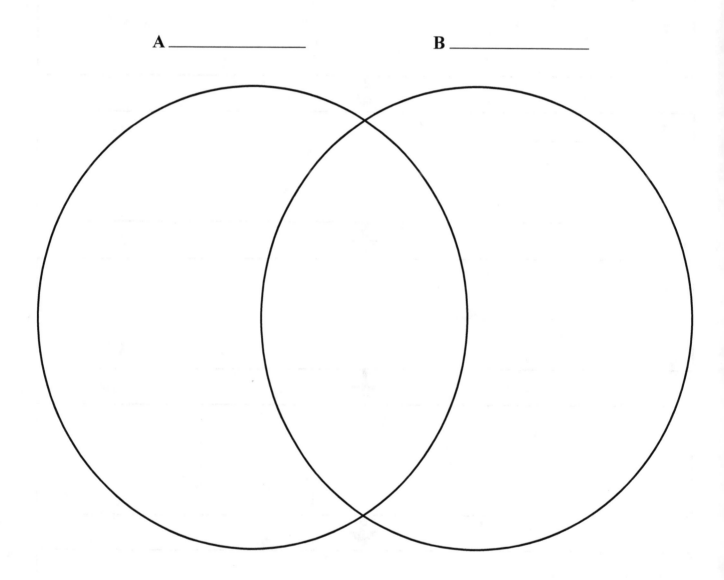

A _____   B _____

120

Problem and Solution Chart

Write the problem in the box below the question mark. Complete the box. Then write the solution in the box below the light bulb. Complete that box, too.

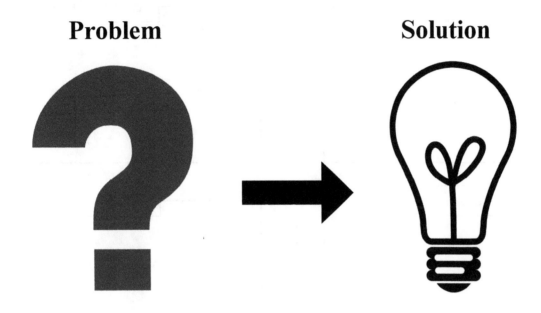

Problem	Solution
Problem	**Solution**
Example	**Why the solution works**
Details	

Cause and Effect Chart

Write what happened in the Effect box. Write the reason it happened in the Cause box.

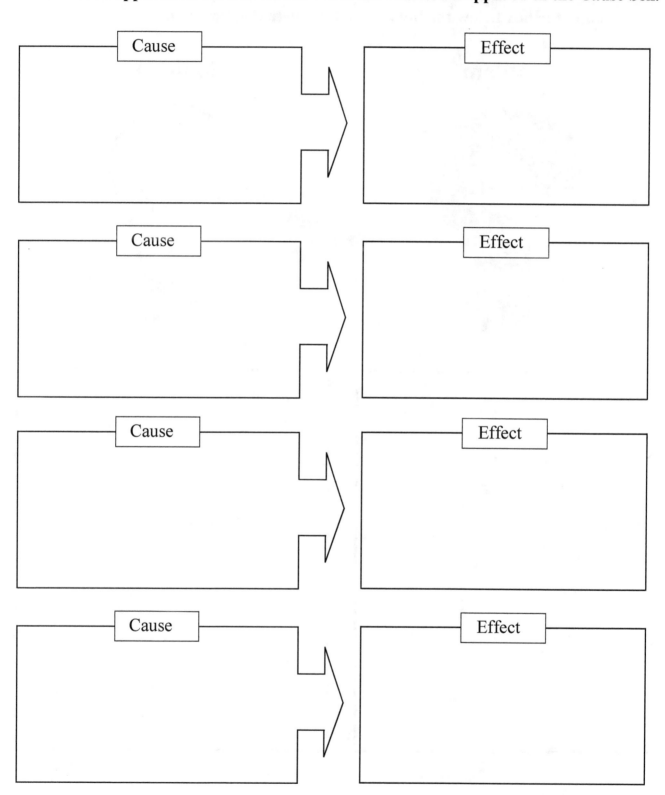

Summary Chart

Write the details on the left side of the chart. Write a summary on the right side of the chart. Try to include all the information in as few sentences as you can.

Who	Summary
	_____
	_____
What	_____
	_____
	_____
Where	_____
	_____
	_____
When	_____
	_____
	_____
Why	_____
	_____
	_____
How	_____
	_____

123

Note Cards

Topic _____

Question _____

Title _____

Author _____

Name of magazine, encyclopedia, atlas, etc. _____

_____

Pages _____

Notes _____

_____

_____

Topic _____

Question _____

Title _____

Author _____

Name of magazine, encyclopedia, atlas, etc. _____

_____

Pages _____

Notes _____

_____

_____

Glossary

active voice (page 31) a sentence in which the subject does the action

adjective (page 8) a word that describes a noun or pronoun; tells how something looks and feels or how many

adverb (page 9) a word that describes a verb, an adjective, or another adverb; shows where, when, or how

antonym (page 37) a word that means the opposite of another word

audience (page 2) the ones who will read what you write

biography (page 99) a true story of someone's life

book report (page 90) a report that tells about the important parts of a book

brainstorming (page 12) thinking about ideas for what you will write

cause (page 64) why something has happened

cause and effect writing pattern (page 64) a writing pattern that tells a cause and an effect

character (page 27) a real or made-up person or animal in a story

comma (page 27) a mark of punctuation that signals a pause

command (page 26) a sentence that gives an order or a direction

common noun (page 5) a word that names any person, place, or thing; begins with a lowercase letter

compare (page 62) to tell how two things are alike

compare and contrast writing pattern (page 62) a writing pattern that tells how two things are alike and different

concluding sentence (page 50) the last sentence in a paragraph that says the main idea in different words

contrast (page 62) to tell how two things are different

conventions (page 16) the rules of grammar and spelling; a writing trait

descriptive paragraph (page 70) a paragraph that describes a person, place, or thing

details (page 12) facts and information

detail sentences (page 50) the sentences in a paragraph that tell more about the main idea

dialogue (page 27) words characters say

drafting (page 12) writing ideas on paper; a step in the writing process

editing (page 13) correcting mistakes that you have made in writing; a step in the writing process

effect (page 64) what happened

entertain (page 3) to please or amuse the reader

exclamation (page 25) a sentence that shows excitement; it ends with an exclamation mark

exclamation mark (page 25) a mark used at the end of an exclamation

express (page 3) to tell your personal feelings

friendly letter (page 88) a letter sent to someone to tell news the reader wants to hear

future tense (page 7) a verb that tells what will happen in the future

helping verb (page 31) a verb that comes before the main verb in a sentence

homophones (page 38) words that sound alike but have different spellings and meanings

how-to paragraph (page 76) tells how to do something through a sequence of steps

ideas (page 14) the thoughts and pictures you form in your mind; a writing trait

indented (page 49) moved to the right slightly

inform (page 3) to tell facts about a topic

information paragraph (page 80) tells facts about one topic

journal (page 4) a record of daily events

main idea (page 19) the most important idea of the writing

main idea and details writing pattern (page 60) writing pattern that tells the most important idea and uses details to tell more about it

note cards (page 97) cards that are used to write information about a topic

noun (page 5) a word that names a person, place, or thing

opinion (page 78) what someone thinks, feels, and believes; it cannot be proved

organization (page 14) the way you group the ideas you are writing; a writing trait

organize (page 2) to arrange the ideas you are writing

outline (page 98) a graphic organizer that shows the order of information in a report

paragraph (page 49) a group of sentences that tells about one main idea

passive voice (page 31) a sentence in which the subject does not do the action

past tense (page 7) a verb that tells what happened in the past

period (page 23) a mark used at the end of a sentence or an abbreviation

personal narrative (page 68) a story about something you have done

persuade (page 3) to try to get the reader to think or act a certain way

persuasive paragraph (page 78) tries to make the reader do something or think a certain way

plot (page 101) the series of actions in a short story

poem (page 86) a form of writing that shows feelings in a creative way

predicate (page 20) the part of a sentence that tells what the subject is or does

preposition (page 10) a word that shows place or time

present tense (pages 7, 22) a verb that tells what is happening now

presentation (page 16) the way the words and pictures look on a page; a writing trait

Glossary
Core Skills Writing, Grade 3

prewriting (page 12) thinking about what and why you are writing; a step in the writing process

problem (page 63) something that is wrong

problem and solution writing pattern (page 63) a writing pattern that tells what is wrong and how to fix it

pronoun (page 6) a word that takes the place of a noun

proofread (page 13) to look for mistakes you have made in writing

proofreading marks (page 46) special marks used during editing to show how to correct mistakes

proper noun (page 5) a word that names a special person, place, or thing; begins with a capital letter

publishing (page 13) sharing your writing with others; a step in the writing process

purpose (page 3) your reason for writing

question (page 24) a sentence that asks something

question mark (page 24) a mark used at the end of a question

quotation (page 27) a sentence with a quote

quotation marks (page 27) marks placed before and after the exact words a speaker says

quote (page 27) the exact words that someone said

resources (page 96) materials where you find facts

revising (page 13) reading your writing and looking for ways to make it better; a step in the writing process

run-on sentence (page 45) a sentence that has two complete thoughts, and the punctuation is not correct

senses (page 33) seeing, smelling, hearing, tasting, and touching to learn about your world

sentence (page 16) a group of words that tells a complete thought

sentence fluency (page 16) when your sentences flow smoothly and have a rhythm; a writing trait

sequence (page 61) the order of actions or events

sequence of events writing pattern (page 61) a writing pattern that tells the order of actions or events

series (page 42) a list of three or more words or items

setting (page 101) where and when a short story takes place

short report (page 96) a form of writing made up of several paragraphs that give facts about a topic

short story (page 101) a story with several paragraphs that tells about made-up characters

solution (page 63) how something is fixed

statement (page 23) a sentence that tells something; it ends in a period (.)

subject (page 20) the part of a sentence that tells who or what the sentence is about

summary writing pattern (page 65) a writing pattern that tells the most important details

summarizing (page 65) telling the most important details of an event or a piece of writing

synonym (page 36) a word that has almost the same meaning as another word

take notes (page 97) to write information in your own words

tense (page 7) the time a verb tells

time-order words (page 57) transition words that help show sequence

topic (page 12) what you are writing about

topic sentence (page 50) a sentence that tells the main idea of the paragraph

transition words (page 56) words in sentences that help the text flow from one idea to the next

verb (page 7) a word that shows action or a state of being

voice (page 15) the way a writer shares his or her feelings with the reader through writing; a writing trait

word choice (page 15) choosing words to express ideas; a writing trait

writing patterns (page 60) ways to organize your work so a reader can best understand the topic

writing traits (page 14) seven skills that help you reach your purpose for writing

Answer Key

Student answers will vary on the pages not included in this Answer Key. Accept all reasonable answers.

Page 1
1. C
2. A

Page 2
Answers will vary. Possible answers are given
1. teacher
2. neighbor
3. friend
4. young child

Page 3
Answers will vary. Possible answers are given.
1. inform, persuade
2. express, entertain
3. entertain
4. inform

Page 5
Answers will vary. Possible answers are given.
1. playground; Pease Park
2. book; Oak Hill Library
3. board; Go Fish!

Page 6
Answers will vary. Possible answers are given.
1. bed–it; clothes–they
2. Mom–she; Dad–his
3. paper–it; library–its

Page 7
Answers will vary. Possible answers are given.
1. cooking, pouring
2. pedals, rides
3. sweeping, vacuuming

Page 8
Answers will vary. Possible answers are given.
1. white, cold, soft
2. red, sweet, tasty
3. smelly, black, white

Page 9
Answers will vary. Possible answers are given.
1. hard, easily, often
2. swiftly, forever, there
3. loudly, angrily, sometimes

Page 11
1. Students should use *and*.
2. Students will probably use *because*.
3. Students should use *or*.

Page 13
Order: 2, 4, 1, 5, 3

Page 14
1. sentence
2. traits
3. idea
4. organization

Page 15
1. senses
2. words
3. voice

Page 16
1. presentation
2. title
3. conventions
4. fluency

Page 17
1. list
2. interest
3. picture
4. topic

Page 18
1. best
2. draft
3. stick
4. out loud

Page 19
1. title
2. mistakes
3. picture

Page 21
1. The fluffy cat. | Answers will vary.
2. Answers will vary. | happily chirped.
3. Answers will vary. | slithered in the grass.

Page 31
1. Children sang the songs.
2. We eat the food.

Page 34
1. fog, blanket; Both things cover an area.
2. umbrella, tree; Both are in the air and spread out.
3. boat, knife; Both things move across a thing to separate it.
4. moon, Grandma's smile; Both were big, bright, and shiny.

Page 38
1. There was one woh week weak left before the big race.
2. Vida could not knot wait weight for four the day to two come.
3. She had practiced so sew hard.
4. Vida knew new that she would wood be the one woh to win the race!

Page 39
1. The chicken danced and sang.
2. The barnyard animals stood up and clapped.
3. The chicken decided to put on a show and travel around the world.

Page 40
1. The moon and stars lit up the night sky.
2. Some crickets and birds sang.
3. Neisha and Laura smiled at the sounds.

127

Page 41

1. Ray heard a noise, but he did not know where it came from.
2. The noise could have come from under his bed, or it could have come from his closet.
3. Ray opened his closet, and he looked inside.

Page 42

1. The fall leaves are red, orange, and yellow.
2. Jan, Mother, and Dad rake the leaves.
3. Ken can rake, bag, or mulch the leaves.

Page 45

Answers will vary. Possible answers are given.
1. Pat got out a glass, and she filled it with water.
2. Pat tapped the glass with a spoon. She liked the sound
3. She drank some of the water. Pat tapped the glass again.
4. Pat filled glasses with different amounts of water. Then she played a tune.

Page 46

1. Dr⊙ tooth is my dentist⊙
2. I went to visit her on tuesday⊙
3. She ^cleaned ~~elen8d~~ my teeth ^, ^and she flossed my teeth⊙
4. When was the last time that you went ^to ~~to8~~ the Ɖentist ^?

Page 49

Main idea: A frog can live on land and in water.
Details: Students write any two details from the paragraph.

Page 50

1. Students underline: *Hot chocolate is a great drink to have on a cold, dark day.*
2. Students show the following numbering:
   1. *The hot cup warms my hands.*
   2. *The rising steam warms my face.*
   3. *When I drink it, the hot chocolate warms me on the inside from my head to my toes.*
   4. *But the best part is the melted marshmallow.*
   5. *The white goo sticks to the tip of my nose and lip.*
   6. *It looks like I have a marshmallow mustache.*
   7. *It makes me laugh.*
3. Students circle: *The hot chocolate makes the day a little brighter.*

Page 51

Order: 3, 2, 1, 5, 4

Page 55

Sentence order may vary.

<u>The Fourth of July is a fun holiday.</u> Many towns have parades. People display the U.S. flag. Family and friends get together. They have picnics in the park. And best of all, fireworks light up the night sky!

Page 56

Answers will vary. Possible answers are given

Watermelon is a great fruit to eat on a hot summer day. The sweet flavor bursts on my tongue. The juice drips down my chin. It ^also falls on my clothes. ^Sometimes I get several seeds in my mouth. You better watch out! I can spit them really far!

Page 57

Order: 1, 5, 3, 6, 4, 2

Making a pizza is easy. First, you spread out the dough to make the crust. Then, you spread tomato sauce on the crust. Next, you add your favorite toppings, like cheese and tomatoes. Finally, you bake it. However, the easiest part is eating the pizza!

Page 58

Answers will vary. Possible answers are given.
1. myself
2. people in the community, adults
3. teenagers, friends, adults
4. children
5. family members, friends

Page 101

1. Goldilocks, Papa Bear, Mama Bear, Baby Bear
2. long ago, in the woods
3. Goldilocks enters the Bears' house and makes herself at home.
4. Possible answer: Goldilocks sits in all three chars and breaks Baby's chair.
5. Goldilocks runs out of the house when the Bears wake her up.

Printed in the USA
CPSIA information can be obtained
at www.ICGtesting.com
LVHW081259160823
755279LV00014B/469